MOORISH

MOORISH

BEN TISH

WITH PHOTOGRAPHY BY
KRIS KIRKHAM

BLOOMSBURY ABSOLUTE
LONDON • OXFORD • NEW YORK • NEW DELHI • SYDNEY

INTRODUCTION

I've been submerged in the cuisine and food culture of Spain and Italy for well over a decade. In that time I've explored the many regions of these magnificent countries getting to know their markedly different culinary styles. In particular I've become more and more intrigued by those regions where the Moors left their influence. I've learnt how and where they stamped their mark and enjoyed finding out how they managed to combine the indigenous produce and ingredients of the region with their own imported techniques, flavourings, ingredients and spicing to produce the exotic, full-flavoured and vibrant cuisine that we know today. In this book I have set out to explore and celebrate the culinary influence that followed the Muslim conquest of the Iberian peninsula, southern Italy and Sicily.

The invading Berbers of North Africa and later the Arabs from the Middle East were known colloquially as Moors, a catch-all description used to cover the colonial Muslim rulers. The Moors shaped and moulded the infrastructure of the Iberian peninsula, transforming the region's religion, architecture, science, art and food. The legacy of the Moors has lived on long after their expulsion in the late 15th century and can still be seen in the cities, towns and villages to this day. And while many of the physical structures have faded over time, the cuisine is still as bright and as vibrant as ever.

The Moors brought with them exotic spices, fruits, vegetables and nuts. Big, bold-flavoured dishes were created, combining the sun-soaked exotic tastes of North Africa and the Arabic world with the foods and produce of the region. Over time the sacred mixed happily with the profane as dishes built around the forbidden European foods of pork and shellfish were married with the spices and sauces of the Muslim East.

The oppressed Jewish population of Andalucía and southern Spain sided with the Arabs after the invasions in 711. Jews from all over the Mediterranean flocked to Andalucía, attracted by the new, vibrant and exciting era of Spain's golden age. Jewish-Moorish cuisine produced wonderful dishes such as partridge cooked and stuffed with coriander, eggs, pine nuts and almonds, and an exotic celebratory dish that was comprised of a complex layering of omelettes, meatballs, mincemeat, aromatic spices and rose water – the dish then left to cook overnight on Friday ready for the Saturday sabbath.

These were wonderfully exciting times for this most extraordinary melting pot of cultures and cuisines. A halcyon period for food emerged as Jewish and Spanish dishes took on Moorish influences and were refined and reinterpreted. Simple peasant dishes soon became indulgent Arabic creations.

I've divided this book into chapters based around the way that I like to cook at home. Super fresh, light refreshingly delicious dishes; slow-cooked dishes that can be left all day to do their thing, filling the house with evocative scents of the East; barbecue and grill dishes that work brilliantly with Moorish inspired spices and flavourings; a sweet and sour chapter celebrating my favourite flavour combination; breakfast and brunch dishes that will make you think again about how you start your day; a short chapter on drinks, long on flavour and deep in alcohol.

First and foremost this is a book for the home cook. The recipes included are in the main simple, though there are a few that will take a little more time than others. And there are also a few recipes that include the occasional ingredient that will need sourcing from specialist food shops or from online stores.

While the recipes included are steeped in authenticity, they more often than not include my own twists and interpretations, influenced by my travels around the region. These are recipes that have been developed and finessed in my kitchen at home, all the while holding firm to the extraordinary influences and techniques of the Moors of the Iberian peninsula.

In short, my book, which is now your book, is all about great, bold, wonderful flavours. The flavours of the Mediterranean and the Moors – Moorish.

Ben Tish
London, 2019

N
S

Porto

PORTUGAL

SPAIN

Barcelona

Lisbon

MALLORCA
IBIZA

Valencia

711–18

714

Seville

714

Andalucía

Mediterranean Sea

Algiers

Tangier

Gibraltar

682–83

MOROCCO

Marrakesh

The Route of the Moorish Conquest.

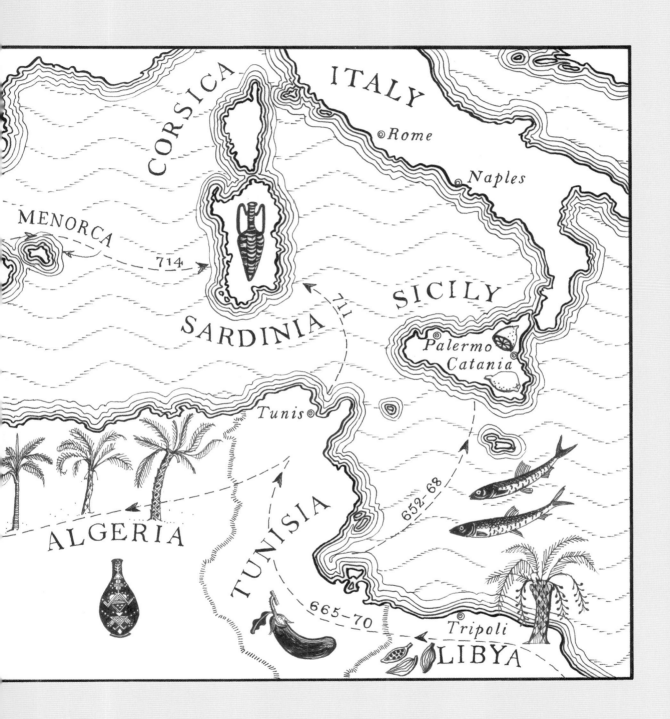

CORSICA

ITALY

◎ Rome

◦ Naples

MENORCA

714

SARDINIA

SICILY

Palermo
Catania

Tunis ◎

ALGERIA

TUNISIA

211

652–68

665–70

Tripoli

LIBYA

Spices

The introduction of spices by the Moors into southern Spain and Italy brought a sparkling culinary enlightenment to the region. A vibrancy of flavours, completely unknown before, soon became an integral part of the make-up of the area's cuisine. As a snapshot of the far-reaching culinary influence of the Moors, Spain now produces 80 per cent of the world's saffron, while the island of Sicily absorbed cumin and cinnamon into many of its savoury and sweet dishes.

Spices have become a passion of mine over recent years and I love spice-heavy cuisines. My wife is half Indian and I've spent a lot of time travelling through Assam, taking back influences from the region to try out in my kitchen at home, experimenting with freshly ground dry spice mixes and pastes.

This book showcases all of my favourite spices – cumin, cinnamon, cardamom, saffron, fennel seeds and sumac, and throughout I explain how best to use them and with which foods they work best, and how some spices are best added at the beginning of a dish and others right at last minute.

I haven't been classically trained in using spices, which is one of the reasons that I find them so magically intriguing. With the potential to be both potent and also subtle, their possibilities in the kitchen are endlessly enticing and challenging. Spices need to be fresh – three-year-old jars at the back of the store cupboard won't do – so be sure to buy little and often, and grind them as and when needed.

Smoked Paprika

Paprika or 'pimentón' was originally introduced into Spain not by the Moors but by the Spanish themselves from Mexico in the 16th century. When the ever-hungry Spaniards found themselves with a happy abundance of flavoursome and juicy red 'pimentón' they quickly jumped on the idea of drying them and turning them into their own paprika de pimentón.

The smoked paprika originated in the region of La Vera in south-west Spain where the rainy climate meant it was hard to air dry peppers so a smoky boost of heat was added! And thus, rather more by luck and necessity than design, the smoked pimentón powder was created, emboldened with rich depth, subtle smoky spice and an intriguing ethereal flavour. This exotic spice instantly became absorbed into the regions of Spain and Portugal where Moorish-influenced cuisine was already prevalent. Smoked pimentón became an instant bedfellow with cumin, coriander and saffron.

Smoked pimentón – both hot and sweet varieties – are used in Spanish chorizo and sobrassada for flavour and colouring as well as in rich stews such as Algerian mutumma and nut-based sauces such as romesco. I love to create dry blackening rubs for meat and fish made with sweet smoked paprika mixed with a little sea salt and honey and some fresh thyme – perfect for cooking over coals or wood. I also love to stir a spoon of hot smoked paprika into white beans or lentils just a few minutes before they have finished cooking.

Smoked paprika is now widely available in varying degrees of quality, often contained within incredibly cool, retro packaging.

Cumin

If there is one spice that epitomises the heady, exotic influences of Moorish cuisine then, for me, it's cumin.

Brought by the Moors from the Middle East to southern Spain, cumin is one of the oldest known spices with links to ancient Egypt, and even garnering a mention in the Hebrew Bible.

Cumin has a warming, curry-like flavour, slightly bitter and rather understated, whilst at the same time able to maintain a wonderful rumbling presence in any dish.

Buy whole seeds to use either as they are or to grind as needed. Cumin is a spice that works really well with many ingredients – lightly broken seeds rubbed over lamb with garlic and chilli for a simple marinade is one of my favourites. Or perhaps eggs fried in olive oil, gently infused with a sprinkling of seeds. Vegetables benefit from a sprinkle of cumin too – roasted beetroots, celeriac, parsnips and potatoes come alive with a little cumin. Or a vinaigrette infused with ground cumin and tossed through leafy greens with lemon.

Where cumin really comes into its own is its use in braises and slow-cooked dishes, especially when added to the base at the start via a soffrito. Or when fried with garlic and onions, the seeds releasing their aromas and gently infiltrating the dish spreading warmth and depth. Try cumin with oxtail, pork shoulder or some meaty monkfish or cod cheeks.

Cumin has become a stalwart in my kitchen, along with salt, pepper and lemon, and so it should be in yours!

BREAKFAST & BRUNCH

I love weekend breakfasts and brunches, and when I have time I'll pull out all the stops. There's something almost sublime about drifting around the kitchen at a leisurely pace, with the day and its many culinary possibilities and expectations still to look forward to. It's also my time to bake bread.

For those who live in the southern Mediterranean, breakfast usually comprises of an incredibly strong double espresso, possibly a very sweet pastry and quite often a couple of cigarettes – not really the breakfast of champions but charmingly endearing and a ritual I fully embrace when on my travels there! My breakfast and brunch recipes feature plenty of eggs and lots of fresh punchy flavours to kick start the day – chillies, coriander-flavoured green harissa, spices such as cumin and coriander seeds, all set alongside sweet, comforting and indulgent dishes like my Crispy Fried Aubergines with Honey (see page 50) or my Pan-fried Fruit Bread with Sticky Stoned Fruits and Cinnamon Cream (see page 22).

Simple basic breads have been around for tens of thousands of years and over time have been refined through the milling of wheat and the development of fermenting. The Arabs were far ahead of their time both in terms of processing and cooking and also in their development of different wheats to produce tastier, lighter breads.

I have included my own favourite Moorish-inspired bread recipes here to kick start your morning and to take you on through the day.

Sicilian Brioche

What is it that makes this brioche Sicilian? Well, it's eaten in Sicily at all times and any time – breakfast, lunch and dinner or in between, filled with granita, gelato or whipped cream and is as ubiquitous as an espresso or a bowl of pasta. The Sicilian version is often lightly spiced with cinnamon and fragranced with citrus zests and orange blossom honey. And of course the Sicilian brioche has the *tuppo* (or peak) adorning the top of the brioche that must be eaten before even thinking about biting into the delicious base.

I recommend that you do as the locals do and stuff them with ice cream, though the rather more restrained addition of a salty soft cheese is also a good choice.

Makes 9

180ml full-cream milk
545g strong white flour, sifted
10g instant dried yeast
1 teaspoon salt
6 tablespoons caster sugar
1 teaspoon ground cinnamon
2 free-range eggs, lightly beaten

75g unsalted butter, melted
1 tablespoon runny honey (preferably orange blossom)
grated zest of ½ orange
grated zest of ½ unwaxed lemon
1 free-range egg beaten with 1 tablespoon milk, for the egg wash

Warm the milk until lukewarm. Put the flour into a free-standing electric mixer fitted with the dough hook. Add the yeast, salt, sugar and cinnamon, then add the beaten eggs, the butter, honey and orange and lemon zests. Mix on the low setting until just combined.

With the mixer still on low speed, gradually add the lukewarm milk. When the ingredients have come together to form a dough, increase the mixer speed to the next setting and beat/knead for about 5 minutes – the dough will start off slightly sticky but do not add more flour to it. When the dough is soft and elastic, transfer to a mixing bowl. Leave to rise in a warm draught-free place (such as the oven with the light on) for 1 hour or until the dough has doubled in size.

Pull off 9 portions of dough weighing 90g each and shape into balls. Place evenly spaced on a baking tray lined with baking parchment. Divide the rest of the dough into 9 portions, each weighing 15g, and shape into balls to make the *tuppo*. Use your thumb to press a deep indentation in each large ball and nestle the *tuppo* in the indentation.

Return to a warm draught-free place to rise for 2–2½ hours or until the brioches are doubled in size.

Preheat the oven to 180°C/160°C fan/Gas Mark 4.

Brush each brioche with the egg wash. Bake in the centre of the oven for about 20 minutes or until the brioche are golden brown.

Allow to cool on a wire rack before serving. My Pomegranate Ripple Ice Cream (see page 220) is great with the brioches or you could try the Almond Granita (see page 209).

Cádiz Molletes

These lovely soft bread rolls are specific to southern Spain. I've tried them in Cádiz where the locals insist they originated, though others say they were created in the Andalucían town of Antequera, where the locals swear blind it's theirs that are original. I love the regional bickering over something as seemingly simple as a bread roll, perfectly highlighting the importance of food to Andalucían culture.

The rolls are eaten for breakfast or afternoon tea, split, drizzled with olive oil and salt and sometimes either rubbed with ripe summer tomatoes or stuffed with jamón.

Makes 8

Starter
100g strong white flour
15g fresh yeast
50ml lukewarm water

Dough
15g fresh yeast
320ml lukewarm water

1 teaspoon sugar
50ml extra virgin olive oil
500g strong white flour, plus extra for dusting
15g fine salt
1 teaspoon ground cinnamon

Make the starter the day before you want to bake the bread. Put the flour on a work surface and make a well in the centre. Dissolve the yeast in the water, then mix into the flour to form a soft, smooth, elastic dough. Shape into a ball and transfer to a bowl. Cover with clingfilm and leave in the fridge for 12 hours to ferment.

The next day, make the dough. Whisk the yeast into the warm water along with the sugar and olive oil. Leave for 10 minutes to activate and become foamy.

Pour the yeast mix into the bowl of a free-standing electric mixer fitted with a dough hook. Add half the flour and the salt and mix together, then add the starter. The mix will be quite wet at this stage. Continue to mix, adding the rest of the flour, then mix/knead for about 10 minutes or until the dough is smooth and elastic. (Alternatively, you can make and knead the dough by hand.)

Transfer the dough to a floured bowl, cover with a tea towel and leave to prove for about 1½ hours or until doubled in size.

Turn the dough out on to a floured surface. Knock back and knead for 3 minutes, then divide into 8 pieces. Roll each piece into a ball and place, well spaced, on a baking sheet lined with baking parchment. Flatten the balls slightly. Cover with a tea towel and leave to prove again for about 30 minutes or until they've increased by about a third in size.

Preheat the oven to 240°C/220°C fan/Gas Mark 9.

Dust the rolls with flour and cinnamon, then bake for about 20 minutes or until they are a pale golden brown (molletes are traditionally pale) and they sound hollow when the base is tapped. Cool on a wire rack.

Pan-fried Fruit Bread
with Sticky Stone Fruits and Cinnamon Whipped Cream

This wonderful dish makes for a very indulgent weekend brunch or a sumptuous dessert over the summer months when stone fruits are in season. I love the subtle flavours of the aromatic spice and the fragrant orange zest coming through the sticky caramelised fruit juices whilst the dollop of cinnamon cream on top brings everything together as it melts into the fruits and the warm fried bread.

Choose firmer stone fruits, although not underripe, as they will cook and caramelise well while holding their shape.

Serves 4

4 apricots, cut in half and
  stone removed
4 firm plums, cut in half and
  stone removed
2 nectarines or firm peaches, cut in
  half and stone removed
175g golden caster sugar
2 tablespoons runny honey
150g unsalted butter, at room
  temperature
2 star anise

1 cinnamon stick
4 sprigs of thyme
grated zest of ½ orange
4 thick slices of fruit bread, such
  as panettone

Cinnamon cream
250ml double cream
40g icing sugar
½ teaspoon ground cinnamon

Preheat the oven to 180°C/160°C fan/Gas Mark 4.

Toss the fruits in a bowl with the caster sugar, honey, half the butter, the spices, thyme and orange zest. Transfer everything to a baking tray, spreading it out into a single layer. Place in the oven and cook for 35–45 minutes or until the fruits have nicely softened and the juices and sugar have become caramelised and sticky. The cooking time will be dependent on the water content and ripeness of the fruits.

While the fruits are in the oven, whip the double cream in a bowl until firm peaks have formed. Quickly whisk in the sugar and cinnamon. Reserve in the fridge.

Remove the fruits from the oven to cool a little while you fry the fruit bread. Do this in 2 batches. Melt half the remaining butter in a large sauté pan until it starts to foam. Add 2 of the bread slices and fry on both sides until golden brown. Drain well on kitchen paper. Repeat with the other 2 slices and remaining butter.

To serve put a slice of fruit bread on each plate and spoon the fruits on top. Drizzle the sticky caramelised juices over the fruits and add a good dollop of cold cinnamon cream.

Portuguese Pão Alentejo
Sourdough

The eponymous bread of the southern Portuguese region of Alentejo – the famous 'bread basket' of Portugal – is much more than a regional bake, it's a symbol of the food culture of the region itself, the country and the whole Iberian peninsula.

An area heavily influenced by the Moorish culture during the occupation, Alentejo is home to one of the first recorded Arab recipes, *tharid*, a bread moistened with stock and olive oil, and then served with meat or vegetables – a preparation still popular today, though now rather lighter and more refined than the Moorish original.

Makes 2 loaves

Starter
200g strong white flour
50g dark rye flour
5g fresh yeast
5g fine salt
175ml lukewarm water

Dough
400g strong white flour, plus
    extra for dusting

100g semolina flour
100g rye flour
15g fine salt
10g caster sugar
5g fresh yeast
400ml lukewarm water

The day before you want to bake the bread, make the starter. Mix together the flours in a bowl and rub in the yeast to make a crumb-like consistency. Add the salt and water and mix well. Knead for 10 minutes or so or until the dough is elastic. Place the dough in a clean bowl, cover with a tea towel and leave in the fridge overnight to ferment.

Scoop the starter into a clean mixing bowl and add all the ingredients for the bread dough. Mix well, then knead the dough until it is soft, smooth and elastic – not sticky. Form the dough into a ball and place in a clean, lightly floured bowl. Cover with a tea towel and leave to rest in a warm spot for 1 hour.

Turn out the dough on to a lightly floured surface and knock back, then shape into a ball again. Place back in the bowl, cover and leave to rest for another hour.

Repeat the knocking back but leave the dough to rest for only 30 minutes. Divide the dough in half and shape each half into a ball.

Flour 2 round wicker proving baskets (or use 2 bowls lined with floured tea towels). Place a ball of dough in each one, seam side down, and cover with a tea towel. Leave in a warm place to prove for 1¼ hours or until doubled in size.

...continued on page 26

Preheat the oven to 240°C/220°C fan/Gas Mark 9. Put a baking tray into the oven to heat up.

Transfer the loaves to a pizza peel or an unrimmed baking sheet. Slash the top of each loaf with a sharp knife. Splash or spray some water into the oven, then slide the loaves on to the hot baking tray and bake for 7 minutes. Turn the oven down to 220°C/200°C fan/Gas Mark 7 and bake for a further 30 minutes or until the loaves are a dark brown and sound hollow when tapped on the base. Cool on a wire rack.

This bread is glorious drizzled with good fresh/green extra virgin olive oil and sea salt.

Pane Cuzanto

In times long past, the seasoned bread of Sicily, Pane Cuzanto, was colloquially known as 'the bread of misery'. Traditionally made from a large freshly baked rustic focaccia-type loaf, the top was cut off and then filled with olive oil, seasoning and spices and anything else that was to hand, the lid then put back on and eaten.

Nowadays it's rather more refined, with the addition of fish, grilled vegetables, cheese, olives and capers, and is definitely no longer a bread of misery but rather one that gives great happiness.

You can either buy a quality focaccia loaf (I suggest one about 800g) or, if the baking spirit moves you, make your own with my simple recipe below.

Serves 5–6

Focaccia (or use 800g shop-bought loaf)
500g strong white flour, plus extra for dusting
5g dried yeast granules
10g fine salt
325ml warm water
1 tablespoon olive oil, plus extra for coating
extra virgin olive oil and sprigs of rosemary, to finish

Filling
1 aubergine, finely sliced lengthways
extra virgin olive oil

150g burrata
12 salted anchovies, chopped
a handful of green Sicilian olives, pitted and roughly chopped
200g ripe tomatoes in season, thinly sliced
a handful of torn basil leaves
100g Tomato, Almond and Chilli Pesto (see page 290)
sea salt and black pepper

If you are making the focaccia, put the flour, yeast, salt and water into the bowl of a free-standing electric mixer fitted with the dough hook. Mix on low speed until everything is fully combined to make a dough, then add the oil and knead with the machine for about 10 minutes or until the dough is smooth and silky. (Alternatively, you can make the dough by hand.) Shape the dough into a ball and coat with a little extra oil. Leave to rise in a clean bowl, covered with clingfilm, until doubled in size, about 1 hour.

Tip the dough on to a floured work surface and press into a rough rectangle. Place in a lightly oiled shallow baking tray, measuring about 26 x 36cm. Press the dough in with your fingers, right into the corners. Now leave to rise again, covered, for about 30 minutes or until the dough looks puffed up and airy.

While the dough is rising, preheat the oven to 240°C/220°C fan/Gas Mark 9. Now use your fingertips to poke deep holes across the whole surface of the dough, almost to the bottom.

...continued on page 28

Drizzle extra virgin olive oil generously (but not swimmingly) over the top and sprinkle with sea salt and rosemary sprigs. Bake for about 10 minutes, then turn the oven down to 200°C/180°C fan/Gas Mark 6 and bake for a further 10 minutes. The focaccia should be light and golden brown. Cool completely before turning out.

For the Pane Cuzanto, preheat the oven to 180°C/160°C fan/Gas Mark 4. Heat a ridged grill pan.

Season the aubergine slices and drizzle with olive oil, then cook on the hot grill pan until charred on both sides and softened. Set the aubergine aside.

Slice the top off the focaccia, cutting it roughly in half. Drizzle both cut surfaces with olive oil and seasoning, then set the top aside. Build up the filling on the cut surface of the bottom part of the loaf. Start with the burrata – spread it all over – followed by the anchovies and then the olives. Toss the tomatoes gently with the basil, pesto and seasoning plus a little more oil, then make a layer of this on top. Finish with the grilled aubergines. Put the top of the focaccia in place and press down.

Place the stuffed focaccia on a baking tray and warm in the oven for 7 minutes. Cut the 'sandwich' through into 5 or 6 pieces and serve.

Chickpea and Spelt Flatbreads

Most countries have a version of a flatbread, a simple bread of convenience with a relatively short proving time. The original versions were just a mix of milled grains and water cooked over an open fire.

This version is something I've been tweaking for years, which produces a lovely bread of texture, full of aromatic spicing. The chickpea flour gives a fresh, almost grassy flavour and the spelt flour helps make the bread pleasingly robust. Great either cooked over a barbecue or on an oiled tray under an overhead grill.

Makes 4–6

1 x 7g sachet dried yeast granules
100ml lukewarm water
2 teaspoons runny honey
250g spelt flour, plus extra for dusting
50g chickpea flour (gram flour)
1 teaspoon cumin seeds

1 teaspoon fennel seeds
2 tablespoons extra virgin olive oil, plus extra for cooking
1 tablespoon plain yoghurt
sea salt and black pepper

Dissolve the yeast in the lukewarm water in a small bowl, then whisk in the honey. Leave to activate for about 10 minutes – the mixture will start to foam slightly when ready.

Meanwhile mix together the flours and seeds in a large bowl and season well. Make a well in the centre of the flour and gradually pour in the yeast mix, mixing with the flour as you go. Add the oil and the yoghurt and mix to form a dough. Turn out on to a floured surface and knead for 5 minutes. Gather the dough into a ball and return to the bowl. Cover with a cloth and leave to rise in a warm spot until doubled in size (this should take 1–1½ hours). The dough will be slightly wetter than traditional bread dough.

When the dough is ready, knock it back in the bowl and divide into 6 pieces. Flour a smooth surface and roll out each piece of dough into a rough circle about 1cm thick. Transfer to a tray, stacking up the dough rounds interleaved with baking parchment.

Prepare a charcoal fire in a barbecue or preheat the grill to maximum.

If you are using a barbecue, brush the breads with oil, then lay them carefully on the grill over the hot coals – they will cook quickly. Once they have puffed up, turn them over using tongs and cook the other side. A little char from the flames is fine and quite authentic. If you are grilling, place the breads on an oiled tray, brush the tops with oil and grill until they are puffed and golden brown. Turn them over and repeat the process.

Serve sprinkled with sea salt.

Tarongia (Sicilian Olive Oil-fried Flatbread)
with Anchovy, Fennel, Dried Tomatoes and Pecorino

From the Aeolian islands off the Sicilian coast, this wonderful bread is not for the faint hearted. The dough is fried in olive oil for a few minutes before the toppings are added and then grilled to finish. It is completely delicious and the toppings can be varied to your liking. A spicy pâté such as nduja with some fresh and bitter chicory leaves and lemon is a delicious alternative, as is the Tomato, Almond and Chilli Pesto on page 290.

The dough will naturally take on the flavour of the olive oil used to deep fry, so be sure to go with a favourite variety.

Serves 6

Dough
240ml lukewarm water
50ml red wine
1 tablespoon extra virgin olive oil
1 tablespoon runny honey
1 x 7g sachet dried yeast granules
425g strong white flour, sifted, plus extra for dusting
grated zest of 1 unwaxed lemon
½ teaspoon fine salt
olive oil

Filling
1 bulb of fennel, cored and finely sliced
75g sun-dried tomatoes packed in oil, drained and roughly chopped
1 red onion, finely sliced
1 fresh red chilli, finely sliced
18 salted anchovies
100g pecorino or caciocavallo, grated
1 tablespoon picked thyme leaves
sea salt and black pepper

First make the bread dough. Put the water, wine, oil and honey in a large mixing bowl. Add the yeast and stir well. Leave to activate and become foamy. Now add a third of the flour, the lemon zest and salt and whisk in to make a smooth batter. Mix in the remaining flour to make a manageable dough.

Transfer the dough to a floured surface and knead for a few minutes or until you have a firm, smooth dough. Shape into a ball, place in a bowl and cover with a cloth. Leave to rise in a warm spot for 45 minutes or until doubled in size.

Cut the dough into 6 equal portions. Roll out each piece into a rough circle. Leave to rest for 15 minutes before cooking.

Heat enough olive oil for shallow frying in a deep pan to 170°C. In batches, carefully lower the breads into the hot oil using a metal spatula or spider and fry for 5–6 minutes or until golden brown on both sides. Remove and drain on kitchen paper. Keep warm.

To make the filling, heat a sauté pan over a medium heat and add a glug of olive oil. Add the fennel and season, then cook for 3 minutes or until softened and browned. Add the tomatoes, onion and chilli, stir and cook for a further 3 minutes. Transfer to a bowl.

Preheat the grill. Divide the fennel and tomato mix among the flatbreads, spreading it over the top, followed by the anchovies and then the cheese. Place under the grill and cook for 3 minutes or until the cheese is melted and golden brown. Sprinkle with thyme and serve.

Sobrassada and Cornmeal Bread

During the Middle Ages, after centuries of Muslim rule, the consumption of pork returned to Spain and its islands. Salchichón and chorizo soon became very popular, making use of all the cheaper cuts of the beast with the addition of heavy spicing to add flavour and to preserve or, in more desperate situations, help disguise meat that was past its best.

The heavily spiced Majorcan pork pâté, sobrassada, is still made in the same way using smoked paprika produced on the island.

The Moors donated their stroke of genius to this recipe by baking rendered lamb and goat fat into the simple unleavened flat breads to add richness and meaty flavour. In this version the principle is continued with pâté being baked into a simple cornmeal bread, giving a spicy richness to an otherwise heavy rustic bread.

Absolutely sublime when served with sheep's or goat's milk cheeses and honey.

Serves 8–10

310g strong white flour, plus extra for dusting

90g polenta (cornmeal), plus extra for the baking tray

2 teaspoons fine salt

2 teaspoons instant dried yeast

170g sobrassada, skin removed and broken into chunks

1 tablespoon extra virgin olive oil, plus extra for oiling the bowl

320ml lukewarm water

1 egg beaten with a little water

Mix together the flour, polenta, salt, yeast and sobrassada in a bowl. Pour in the oil and water and stir with a wooden spoon to form a sticky dough. Dust it with flour and knead in the bowl for 3 minutes, adding a little more flour as you go if the dough is very sticky.

Turn the dough out on to a floured work surface and dust with a little more flour. Continue kneading for about 7 minutes or until smooth and elastic. The sobrassada will have spread throughout the dough, flecking it red. Transfer the dough to an oiled bowl, cover and leave in a warm spot to prove for an hour or so or until doubled in size.

Dust a baking tray with polenta. Turn out the dough on to a floured worktop. Flatten it and knead for 3 minutes or so or until smooth and elastic again. Form the dough into an oval loaf and place on the polenta-dusted baking tray. Cover with clingfilm and leave in a warm spot to prove for 40 minutes or until doubled in size.

Preheat the oven to 220°C/200°C fan/Gas Mark 7.

Using a sharp knife, slash the loaf 2 or 3 times across the top. Brush with the egg wash, then bake for 15 minutes. Turn the oven down to 180°C/160°C fan/Gas Mark 4 and bake for a further 30 minutes or until crusty and golden, and the loaf sounds hollow when tapped on the base.

Cool on a wire rack before eating.

Potato, Honey and Thyme Flatbreads

This flat bread recipe is one that I've been tweaking and updating for a few years now. It's an excellent light bread that is given a chewiness via the addition of potatoes.

You can vary the herbs to finish the bread or, as I like to do, brush with melted butter and then sprinkle over some smoked paprika and ground cumin for a spicy alternative.

Makes 12

Starter
50g strong white flour
50ml lukewarm water
2g dried yeast granules

Dough
500g strong white flour
325g lukewarm water
125g roasted potatoes, crushed

30g runny blossom honey
3.2g dried yeast granules
16g fine salt
semolina flour, for dusting
sea salt, for sprinkling

To serve
extra virgin olive oil and picked
    thyme leaves

The day before, mix together the ingredients for the starter in a bowl. Cover and leave at room temperature overnight to ferment and bubble.

Put the starter and all the ingredients for the bread dough into a free-standing electric mixer fitted with a dough hook (or in a bowl if you are making the bread by hand). Start mixing slowly to bring everything together, then speed up for the last few minutes to make sure everything is fully incorporated. The consistency of the dough should be very sticky.

Cover with a cloth and leave to rise at room temperature for an hour or until doubled in size. Knock back, then turn out on to a floured surface and knead for 2–3 minutes before returning to the bowl for a second rise of another hour.

Remove the dough from the bowl and divide into 12 balls, each weighing 100g. Place on a tray lined with baking parchment and leave at room temperature for 30 minutes. Then flatten the balls to about 1.5cm thick. Sprinkle these flatbreads with semolina flour and sea salt. Leave for another 30 minutes before cooking.

The flatbreads are best cooked on a ridged grill pan over a medium heat or over a medium charcoal fire in a barbecue. Lightly drizzle extra virgin olive oil over both sides of the breads and rub in. Cook in batches, carefully lifting the breads up and laying them on the griddle or barbecue grill. They will cook quite quickly – about 3 minutes on each side or until they are browned and puffed up. Serve hot, drizzled with more olive oil and fresh thyme leaves.

Prawn Revuelto
with Wild Garlic and Roast Pepper

Scrambled eggs are such a good vessel for the carrying of delicious things. Revuelto isn't usually eaten for breakfast in Spain – the Spaniards are serious egg lovers and save this dish for the more esteemed eating hours of lunch or dinner.

I like to use tinned, wood-roasted and hand-peeled piquillo peppers for this recipe, still retaining flecks of charred skin with a lovely smoky flavour. You can buy them online or in Spanish delis. Regular jarred peeled peppers are a great substitute.

Serves 4

8 free-range eggs
75ml full-cream milk
50g unsalted butter
olive oil
½ teaspoon sweet smoked paprika
½ teaspoon cumin seeds,
  lightly crushed
12 large raw tiger prawns,
  peeled, deveined if necessary
  and roughly chopped

100g roasted, peeled red peppers
  from a jar (such as piquillo),
  roughly chopped
a handful of wild garlic leaves (if not
  in season use a handful of baby
  spinach leaves plus 1 garlic clove,
  finely chopped)
sea salt and black pepper

Break the eggs into a bowl, add the milk and season with salt and pepper. Whisk well.

Heat a medium non-stick sauté pan over a medium heat and add the butter and a glug of olive oil. When the butter has melted and started to bubble, add the paprika and cumin (and chopped garlic if using spinach) and cook for a minute, stirring. Turn the heat to low and add the egg mixture and prawns. Cook gently, stirring constantly, for 3–4 minutes or until the eggs just start to scramble and the prawns are cooked through.

Add the peppers and wild garlic (or spinach) and cook, mixing well, for a further minute or so to wilt the leaves and warm the peppers through. The eggs should still be quite loose (the residual heat will continue cooking the eggs through).

Immediately transfer the eggs to serving plates. This is great with some home-made flatbread (see page 36).

Potato, Honey and Thyme Flatbreads (see page 36)
Prawn Revuelto with Wild Garlic and Roast Pepper (see page 37)

Gypsy Eggs

I love this warming, comforting brunch dish, and I've been cooking it for many years now, often with a slight hangover. This is my version where the smoked paprika-scented spices and smokiness gently infuse the soft yolk making you feel whole again.

Serves 4

olive oil
1 onion, finely chopped
2 garlic cloves, finely chopped
1 teaspoon hot smoked paprika
½ teaspoon dried chilli flakes
180g spicy cooking chorizo, peeled and cut into chunks
4 slices of jamón serrano, cut into strips

2 x 400g good-quality canned chopped tomatoes
120g frozen peas, thawed
4 large free-range eggs
a few picked coriander leaves
sea salt and black pepper

Preheat the oven to 180°C/160°C fan/Gas Mark 4.

Heat a medium saucepan over a medium heat. Add a glug of olive oil and then the onion and garlic. Cook for 2 minutes. Add the paprika, chilli flakes, chorizo and jamón. Continue to cook, stirring occasionally, for 4 minutes or until the onion has softened and the chorizo juices have been released. Add the chopped tomatoes and simmer until reduced by about half, stirring from time to time.

Divide the tomato-chorizo sauce among 4 ovenproof cocotte dishes. Sprinkle the peas over the sauce and crack an egg on to the top of each dish. Bake for 12 minutes or until the egg white is set but the yolk still soft.

Sprinkle with coriander leaves and serve immediately, with warm flatbreads.

Duck Egg
with Green Harissa and Jamón Ibérico

This is basically egg and bacon Andalucían-style with a little Moorish twist.

Green harissa is a wonderful fresh and spicy chilli-herb paste that when used in this recipe cuts through the richness of the eggs and jamón, balancing out the dish to make it perfection on a breakfast plate.

I like to use jamón Ibérico de bellota, the king of Spanish cured hams but jamón serrano will do the job nicely should Ibérico be hard to find.

Serves 4

4 duck eggs
a splash of white wine vinegar
extra virgin olive oil
120g thinly sliced jamón Ibérico
    de bellota
4 slices of sourdough bread, drizzled
    with olive oil on both sides and
    charred on a ridged grill pan
sea salt and black pepper

Green harissa
65g flat-leaf parsley, leaves picked and
    roughly chopped

30g coriander, leaves picked and
    roughly chopped
2 green chillies, roughly chopped
1 teaspoon ground coriander
1 teaspoon ground cumin
½ teaspoon ground cardamom
grated zest of 1 unwaxed lemon
¼ teaspoon caster sugar
1755ml extra virgin olive oil

First make the harissa. Put all the ingredients into a blender and blitz to a rough purée. Season to taste and reserve.

Crack each egg into a separate small bowl.

Set a medium pan of water over a medium heat, add the vinegar and bring to a simmer. Carefully slide in the eggs from their bowls and cook for about 4 minutes or until the whites are nicely set but the yolk is still soft. Remove from the water with a slotted spoon, drain well on kitchen paper and gently dab dry. Season.

Place an egg on each plate and drizzle over some olive oil. Drape a slice of jamón over the egg and spoon around the harissa. Serve with the grilled sourdough.

Poached Eggs
with Grilled and Marinated Wild Mushrooms and Jamón

One of my favourite spins on the classic Spanish 'jamón and eggs'. I like to use a griddle pan (or better still a barbecue) and grill the fleshy mushrooms for an almost meat-like quality.

It's widely overlooked that the more robust and sturdy lettuces can be cooked with lovely results.

Serves 4

200g meaty king oyster or
    porcini mushrooms, trimmed
    and wiped clean
olive oil
1 garlic clove, finely chopped
2 teaspoons picked rosemary
    leaves, chopped
1 tablespoon sweet sherry vinegar
1 head red chicory, stalk trimmed
1 head yellow/white chicory,
    stalk trimmed

1 large Baby Gem lettuce,
    stalk trimmed
a splash of white wine vinegar
4 free-range eggs
2 teaspoons pine nuts, toasted
40g thinly sliced jamón Ibérico
    de bellota
sea salt and black pepper

Cut the mushrooms in half lengthways (or smaller pieces if the mushrooms are very large) and check again to be sure they are clean – a quick wash under cold running water is okay. Pat dry if washed. Toss the mushrooms with olive oil and seasoning.

Heat a ridged grill pan. Cook the mushrooms over a medium heat until they are tender and nicely charred on both sides. Transfer to a bowl and add the garlic, rosemary, sherry vinegar and a splash of olive oil. Toss the hot mushrooms to mix with the seasonings, then leave to marinate at room temperature for at least 20 minutes. (Keep the grill pan over the heat.)

Meanwhile, separate the leaves of the chicory and lettuce. Put into a bowl with seasoning and some olive oil and toss together. Cook the leaves briefly on the hot grill pan to wilt and lightly char – you'll need to do this in 2 or 3 batches. Transfer to a plate to cool.

Bring a medium pan of water to a simmer and add the white wine vinegar. Carefully slide in the eggs and cook until soft poached. Lift out with a slotted spoon and drain briefly on kitchen paper.

Divide the wilted chicory and lettuce among 4 plates. Spoon the mushrooms with some of the marinade over the chicory-lettuce on each plate and place an egg on top. Finish with toasted pine nuts and slices of jamón. A perfect brunch.

Flamenco Eggs and Pancetta

Shakshuka is a popular Middle Eastern dish with its origins in Tunisia. It is essentially a baked egg dish with tomatoes, peppers, garlic and fresh herbs. The Moorish-Andalucían version is known as flamenco eggs and though quite similar to the Arab version, includes spicy chorizo and jamón.

Hugely popular in the UK and elsewhere as a great breakfast or brunch dish, in Spain and the Middle East it's more likely to be eaten in the evening. Whether served at breakfast or dinner it's always delicious.

Serves 4

olive oil
1 onion, finely sliced
1 red pepper, deseeded and diced
1 green pepper, deseeded and diced
80g smoked pancetta, diced
4 garlic cloves, crushed
2 teaspoons sweet smoked paprika
1 teaspoon cumin seeds
1 teaspoon cayenne pepper

750g quality canned chopped
   tomatoes (or ripe tomatoes
   in season)
2 teaspoons caster sugar
4 large free-range eggs
a small handful of coriander,
   roughly chopped
sea salt and black pepper

Heat a good glug of olive oil in a large, wide pan over a medium heat and add the onion. Cook until golden, then add the peppers and pancetta. Fry until the peppers are soft and the pancetta has released its fat, then stir in the garlic and spices. Cook for 3 minutes.

Pour in the tomatoes and roughly mash. Stir in the sugar. Bring to the boil, then turn down the heat and simmer for 30 minutes. Season to taste and add more cayenne, if needed.

Make 4 indentations in the tomato sauce and break an egg into each. Season them lightly. Turn the heat down to very low, cover with the lid and cook for about 10 minutes or until the eggs are just set – you ideally want the yolks still runny. Sprinkle with the coriander and serve at the table in the pan to share.

Serve with my Sobrassada and Cornmeal Bread (see page 34).

Morcilla and Fried Eggs
with Potatoes and Caramelised Onions

Morcilla is the hugely popular blood sausage found all over Spain and exemplifies Spain's food culture where nothing from the animal goes to waste. It is a centuries old preparation created through extreme poverty in frugal times and long before the Moors arrived.

The Arab influence can be felt in the morcilla of southern Spain and the Balearics where ingredients such as cinnamon, cumin, dried fruits and nuts are added for flavour and as a filler. All good Spanish delicatessens will sell a selection of morcilla.

Serves 4

2 medium Desiree potatoes, peeled and cut into 2cm dice
1 Spanish onion, finely sliced
olive oil
200g spiced southern Spanish morcilla, in sausage-style links

4 free-range eggs
¼ teaspoon hot smoked paprika
sea salt and black pepper

Cook the potatoes in boiling salted water until half cooked. Drain well and lay them out on a tray to steam dry.

Preheat the oven to 190°C/170°C fan/Gas Mark 5.

Toss the potatoes and onion in plenty of olive oil and seasoning, then spread them on a baking tray. Roast, turning them over occasionally with a spatula, for 45 minutes to 1 hour or until the potatoes are golden brown and the onions are nicely caramelised.

About 25 minutes before the potatoes are ready, heat a large, non-stick sauté pan over a medium heat and add a glug of olive oil. Fry the morcilla to brown on all sides. Transfer them to the tray with the potatoes and onions and finish the cooking process. The fat and juices from the morcilla will combine deliciously with the potatoes and onions.

Add some more oil to the pan you fried the morcilla in and gently fry the eggs as you like. Finish them with some seasoning and a sprinkle of smoked paprika. Serve the eggs on top of the sausage and potato.

Crispy Fried Aubergines
with Honey

Aubergines were a gift from the Moors bestowed on the Mediterranean during their occupation. I associate the Mediterranean aubergine with Sicily in particular where it takes centre stage in a whole wonderful variety of dishes, such as the Sicilian signature pasta dish of spaghetti *alla Norma*, in rolled involtini stuffed with raisins, pine nuts and bread or the glorious stuffed aubergines with preserved lemon and almonds on page 103.

This is an incredibly simple recipe and one of my favourite ways to cook the aubergine – deep-fried in a light batter, crispy on the outside, soft and melting within. It's perfect as part of a brunch feast or a pre-dinner snack, and a great accompaniment to the grilled fennel crusted sardines on page 116.

I like to use a deep, intense chestnut honey for this recipe but any quality runny honey will do.

Serves 4

2 medium aubergines (very firm with shiny and unblemished skin)
50g plain flour, sifted
75ml lukewarm water

vegetable oil, for deep-frying
20ml chestnut or other runny honey
1 teaspoon picked thyme leaves
sea salt and black pepper

Trim the ends from the aubergines and discard, then cut the aubergines across into 1cm slices.

Whisk together the flour and water with some salt and pepper in a large bowl until smooth, then leave this batter to rest for 10 minutes.

Heat oil in a deep-fat fryer or deep pan to 170°C. Dip the aubergine slices in the batter, then fry until tender and golden brown on both sides – do this in 2 or 3 batches to avoid over-crowding, which would cause the oil temperature to drop; it is important the oil stays hot to crisp the batter. Drain well and season.

Serve drizzled with honey and sprinkled with thyme leaves.

Home-made Goat's Milk Labneh
with Fresh Peas, Broad Beans, Almonds and Mint

A few years back on a trip to Sicily I stopped off for lunch in a beautiful, historic seaside town called Cefalù. The cafés and restaurants were brimming with a myriad of freshly caught fish. I ordered a simple wood-grilled red mullet and a salad on the side – the salad was a revelation.

It was a simple assembly of freshly podded raw peas and beans with the addition of the most pungent mint, chunks of buttery, marcona-like almonds and a dollop of super fresh, tangy goat's curd, or labneh. Popular in Middle Eastern cuisine, labneh is strained yoghurt.

This version comes pretty close to the Sicilian, minus the blazing sun.

Serves 4

70ml extra virgin olive oil
1½ teaspoons caster sugar
juice of 1 lemon
100g podded super fresh peas
75g podded super fresh broad beans,
    grey skins removed
zest of ½ unwaxed lemon
a handful of mint leaves

50g marcona almonds or other quality
    whole almonds, roughly chopped
sea salt and black pepper

Labneh
900g goat's or cow's milk yoghurt (or a
    mix of the two)
½ teaspoon fine salt

First make the labneh. Line a bowl with a large piece of muslin. Pour in the yoghurt, sprinkle in the salt and stir. Bring the muslin up into a tight bundle and tie the ends together with string. Hang the muslin bag over the bowl, or from your kitchen tap over the sink, and leave to drain for 24 hours. After this time the yoghurt will have lost most of its liquid and will be quite thick – the centre may still be a bit creamy, which is fine. Transfer the labneh to a container and keep in the fridge until ready to use.

Whisk together the oil, sugar and lemon juice in a bowl and season well. Stir the peas and beans into the dressing and sprinkle in the zest.

Spoon the labneh on to serving plates. Top with the peas, beans and dressing. Scatter the mint leaves and almonds over the top and serve.

Courgette Flowers
Stuffed with Sheep's Cheese and Mint

Courgette flowers are perfect for stuffing. Very delicate, they need careful handling so as to avoid tearing the petals which hold in the delicious minty cheese stuffing.
They are at their best in the late summertime.

Serves 4 as a starter

50g soft sheep's cheese, at
    room temperature
4 large courgette flowers, stamens
    carefully removed
4 mint leaves
vegetable oil, for deep-frying
100ml runny orange blossom honey
sea salt

Batter
225g plain flour, sifted
2 teaspoons baking powder
1 teaspoon ground cumin
500ml cold sparkling water

First make the batter. Put the flour, baking powder and cumin in a large wide bowl, add the water and whisk until smooth. The consistency of the batter will be quite loose. Cover with clingfilm and leave to rest at room temperature while you prepare the courgette flowers.

Divide the cheese into 4 balls, then very carefully insert one into the cavity in each flower along with a mint leaf. Pull the petals up and lightly twist together to seal in the cheese. Fold the twists to the side of the flower and place twist side down on a tray. Cut a slit into the stalk (the baby courgette), about halfway up (the cut will help the stalk cook more quickly). Chill for 20 minutes to set.

Heat the oil in a deep-fat fryer or deep pan to 180°C.

Remove the flowers from the fridge and place in the batter, turning them to ensure they are fully coated. Carefully place the flowers, one by one, in the hot oil, flower first: submerge the flower head in the oil for a few seconds to seal, then drop fully into the oil. Cook for 3 minutes, turning once, until a light golden brown. Remove from the oil and drain well.

Serve hot, drizzled with honey, seasoned with sea salt and sprinkled with the remaining mint leaves.

Burrata on Sourdough
with Crushed Coriander and Fennel Seeds and Burnt Orange

At the heart of this recipe is the magical combination of ultra creamy, rich burrata married with the crunchy mix of aromatic spices gently nestling against sweetly charred oranges.

Ensure your burrata is super fresh – in southern Italy, where burrata is made, you'll find that the locals won't consume anything that's over 24 hours old. If you can't find burrata then a fresh buffalo mozzarella will do nicely.

As well as making a delicious brunch, I love to serve this as a starter for a mid-summer dinner when there's an exotic, sultry feel in the air.

Serves 4

2 medium, sweet oranges, peeled, pith removed and cut horizontally in half
1 teaspoon caster sugar
1 tablespoon coriander seeds
½ tablespoon fennel seeds
extra virgin olive oil
4 teaspoons white wine vinegar

4 small slices of sourdough bread
4 small burrata (as fresh as can be), at room temperature
a handful of fresh herb fennel or dill, fronds picked
sea salt and black pepper

Sprinkle the cut side of the orange halves with the sugar and rub it in. Set aside for 5 minutes. Heat a medium sauté pan over a medium heat. Put the orange halves in the pan cut side down. Lower the heat slightly and leave the oranges to caramelise, without moving them, for 8–10 minutes or until coloured to a deep, dark caramel – almost burnt. Remove from the heat and leave the oranges to cool in the pan.

Lightly crush the coriander and fennel seeds with a pestle and mortar. Tip into a small saucepan and cover with a tablespoon of olive oil. Heat the seeds and oil over a low heat until the oil starts to bubble and the seeds lightly fizzle. Immediately remove from the heat and add the vinegar and the caramelised orange juices from the sauté pan. Stir to mix.

Heat a ridged grill pan. Drizzle olive oil over both sides of the bread and char on both sides in the hot pan.

Drain the burrata and carefully pat dry with kitchen paper, then season well. Place a burrata with a piece of caramelised orange on each slice of bread. Spoon over the spice-oil dressing and scatter the herbs on top. Serve immediately.

Shrimp and Cumin Fritters
or *Tortillitas*

These deep fried pancakes are ubiquitous in Andalucía, the frying capital of Europe.

Everywhere has its own version, ranging from smart, high-end restaurants to rough and ready street stalls. I've always found the best ones in the food markets of Cádiz and Grenada, served straight from the fryer in brown paper accompanied by an ice-cold Alhambra beer.

Traditionally these would be made with just chickpea flour but I like to add some plain flour to lighten them up a touch.

The tiny raw shrimps used to make these authentic fritters are best found in the frozen aisles of Asian supermarkets – failing that chopped raw frozen prawns will work well too.

Serves 4–6
(makes 16 fritters)

175g tiny peeled raw shrimps or small peeled raw prawns (thawed if frozen)
75g chickpea flour (gram flour)
100g plain flour, sifted
½ teaspoon baking powder
a small glass of white wine

2 spring onions, finely sliced
½ teaspoon cumin seeds, roughly crushed
½ teaspoon sweet smoked paprika
groundnut oil, for frying
lemon, to serve
sea salt

If using tiny shrimps, just make sure the heads are removed. If using larger shrimps or prawns, cut them into chunks.

Put the flours and baking powder into a bowl and whisk in 300ml of cold water and the wine – you want to achieve a batter with the consistency of thick cream. Add the shrimps, spring onions and spices and season with salt. Stir to mix. Set aside to rest for 10 minutes.

Pour about 1cm of groundnut oil into a large sauté pan and place over a high heat. After a few minutes check that the oil is hot by dropping a little batter into it – it should sizzle straightaway.

Mix the batter again, then working in 2 or 3 batches so as not to over-crowd the pan, drop spoonfuls of the batter into the hot oil and spread them lightly with the back of the spoon to form thin fritters. Cook for 2–3 minutes or until they puff up, turning them so they are nicely browned on both sides with crisp edges.

Remove from the pan straight on to kitchen paper to drain. Sprinkle liberally with salt and serve immediately with lemon wedges to squeeze over. I like to serve these with my Almond Alioli (see page 282).

Chickpea Pancakes (Panelle)
with Cumin, Coriander and Raw Fennel

Palermo is famed for its street food culture and if you take a walk around its narrow streets you'll see, hear and smell the *friggitorie*, or fry shops, in full swing, busily churning out wonderful potato croquettes, fried aubergines and chickpea pancakes.

The panelle pancakes are made with gram chickpea flour, spices and water to form a batter and then fried, often served stuffed inside a sesame-seeded durum wheat bread bun. These tasty pancakes are one of the few chickpea flour-based specialties found in Sicilian cuisine and originate from the time of Arab rule in the 10th century.

My version includes a fresh, crunchy fennel salad.

Serves 4

Pancakes
225g chickpea flour (gram flour), sifted
1 teaspoon ground cumin
½ teaspoon ground cinnamon
½ teaspoon dried chilli flakes
a small handful of coriander, leaves picked and roughly chopped
olive oil, for greasing

vegetable oil, for shallow-frying
4 sesame-seeded buns, split in half
sea salt and black pepper

Salad
1 small bulb of fennel with fronds
juice of ½ lemon
40ml extra virgin olive oil

Whisk together the flour and 750ml of water to make a smooth batter and season well with salt and pepper. Heat a small pan over a medium heat, add the cumin, cinnamon and chilli flakes and toast lightly until fragrant. Add to the batter and stir in along with the chopped coriander.

Pour the batter into a saucepan and cook over a medium heat, stirring constantly, until the batter thickens and comes away from the side of the pan.

Grease a 25 x 10cm baking tin with olive oil. Pour in the cooked batter (you ideally want a depth of about 5mm) and leave to cool completely before placing in the fridge to chill until set.

Make the salad shortly before serving. Finely slice the fennel on a mandoline or with a very sharp knife, then toss with the lemon juice, olive oil and seasoning to taste. Set aside.

Turn the tin upside down to unmould the chickpea cake. Cut it into 5 x 2cm rectangles. Heat the vegetable oil in a pan for shallow-frying to 170°C.

Working in batches, carefully drop the chickpea rectangles into the hot oil and fry until golden brown. Drain well on a tea towel or kitchen paper. Season with sea salt, then serve hot in the buns with the fennel salad.

Patatas Bravas

If there's a signature dish of Spain it probably has to be patatas bravas, found in every tapas bar up and down the country.

The Moorish connection here isn't the dish as a whole but just the sauce – potatoes didn't hit Spain until the 16th century, long after the Moors had been pushed out of the country back to North Africa.

Originating in Madrid as a simple tomato sauce with lots of chilli flakes (*bravas*, roughly translated, means fierce) it then made its way around Spain's regions and picked up its Moorish influence through Andalucía – it's the ultimate version, spicy, smoky and sharpened up with good sherry vinegar. Serve with a large dollop of my home-made alioli on page 282.

Serves 4

600g large waxy potatoes, peeled
 and cut into thick chips
extra virgin olive oil
1 onion, finely chopped
2 garlic cloves, finely chopped
½ fresh red chilli, finely chopped
1 tablespoon hot smoked paprika
1 heaped teaspoon cumin seeds

1 x 400g can chopped tomatoes
250g very ripe tomatoes, cored
 and roughly chopped
1 tablespoon sherry vinegar
1 teaspoon picked thyme leaves
Alioli (see page 282), to serve
sea salt and black pepper

Rinse the potatoes in cold water, then place them in a pan of salted water. Bring to a simmer and partly cook – they should still be a little firm in the centre. Drain and spread the potatoes on a tray to cool for at least 1 hour.

To make the sauce, heat a glug of olive oil in a medium saucepan over a medium heat. Add the onion, garlic, chilli, smoked paprika and cumin seeds. Cook, stirring frequently, for 4 minutes or until the onion is very soft. Add the canned and fresh tomatoes and the vinegar. Bring to the boil, then simmer gently for an hour or so until the sauce has reduced by half, stirring occasionally to prevent it sticking. Season well and stir in the thyme leaves plus a splash of oil. Remove from the heat.

Preheat the oven to 200°C/180°C fan/Gas Mark 6. Tip the potatoes into a roasting tray. Liberally drizzle olive oil over them and toss to coat. Season well. Roast, shaking the tray occasionally, for 45 minutes or until the potatoes are crisp and golden brown.

Sprinkle the potatoes with sea salt and spoon the bravas sauce on top. Serve with the alioli on the side.

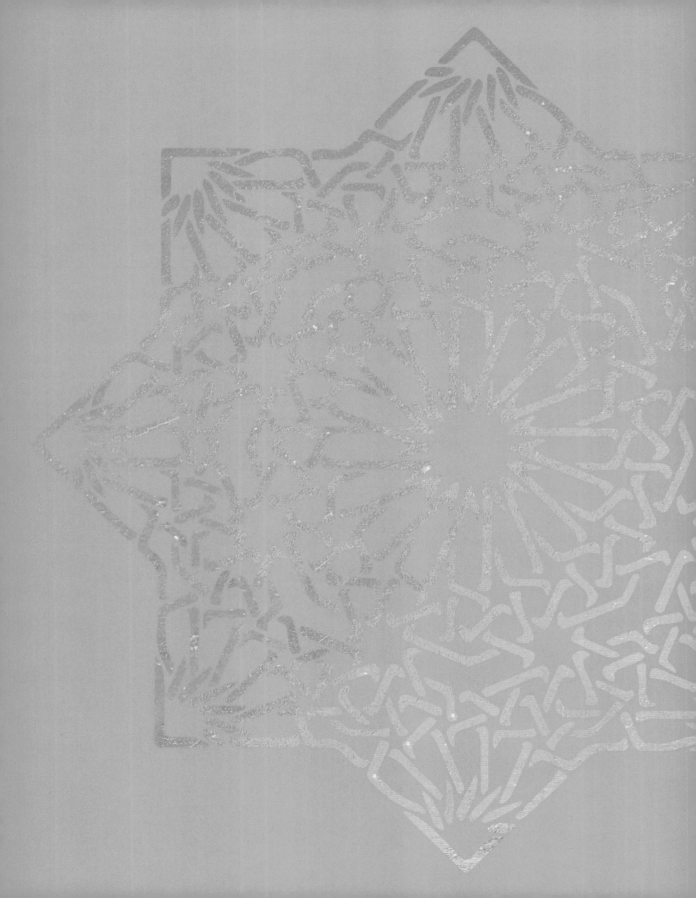

FRESH

I am an evangeliser for all things fresh and vibrant in food. The Moorish settlement and colonisation of southern Europe brought with it both an amazingly innovative approach to fresh eating and also a new understanding of the produce they found close at hand.

Fresh produce and how to enjoy it was a priority. The freshest of fish was eaten either raw or lightly cooked using acidity to gently cure. Vegetables were served chilled, punchily dressed with vibrantly flavoured sauces to enliven the palate and combat the sweltering heat of the southern Mediterranean summers. The chilled salmorejo and gazpacho soups of Andalucía are classic examples originating from the Moorish occupation which show the inventive ways the Moors utilised the tomato gluts at the season's end. Sicily has a type of sushi-crudo that uses the freshest of fish and shellfish, served cold, lightly cured with sea salt, citrus and herbs.

All the recipes in this section are a testament to my own love of fresh food – just picked vegetables, fish caught less than a day from swimming in the sea or eggs laid by happy chickens just a few hours ago.

My Salmorejo

The potential of a salmorejo to refresh and delight on a hot summer's day is infinite. A simple ice-cold soup made with tomatoes bursting at the seams with ripeness, emulsified with extra virgin olive oil and sherry vinegar, a little day-old bread to thicken and that's it. I like to serve it with thinly sliced jamón Ibérico, soft-boiled eggs and some crunchy, fried migas.

Top-quality ingredients are always important but here they are vital – choose your favourite olive oil as its flavour will play a big part in the taste of the soup, as will the sweetness and juiciness of the tomatoes.

Serves 4

about 800g very ripe vine tomatoes
2 garlic cloves
50ml sherry vinegar
80g day-old sourdough bread, torn into pieces
100ml extra virgin olive oil, plus extra for drizzling
sea salt and black pepper

To serve
2 free-range eggs
50g day-old sourdough bread, any crust removed, ripped into small chunks
olive oil
½ teaspoon picked thyme leaves
50g thinly sliced jamón Ibérico

Bring a large pan of water to the boil and prepare a large bowl of iced water. Remove the stalks from the tomatoes along with the 'eyes', then prick the base of each tomato with the tip of a small knife. Plunge the tomatoes into the boiling water and leave for 30 seconds, then remove with a slotted spoon and plunge into the iced water to refresh. Peel the skins from the tomatoes and quarter them.

Put the tomatoes into a blender with the peeled garlic and a good amount of salt and pepper. Blitz for 2 minutes. Add the vinegar and bread and continue blitzing until you have a smooth purée. With the machine running, slowly pour in the olive oil to emulsify into the tomato base. The mix should look creamy and be very smooth. Transfer the salmorejo to a bowl and check the seasoning before chilling for at least 2 hours.

Soft-boil the eggs (4 minutes from boiling), then cool them in iced water to stop the cooking process. Peel and cut in half lengthways.

Fry the bread chunks in olive oil until golden brown. Tip on to kitchen paper. Season these croutons well and sprinkle with the thyme.

Divide the salmorejo among serving bowls. Place an egg half in the middle of each, add the jamón slices and scatter the croutons on top. Finish with a drizzle of extra virgin olive oil and serve.

Braised Courgettes
with Tomato, Fenugreek, Sheep's Curd and Migas

I love the fragrant, curry-like flavour that fenugreek seeds release when cooked in hot oil – an exotic, complex, almost other-worldly taste that transports you to far off places and cuisines.

First cultivated in the Middle East, fenugreek was brought over to Europe around 1200. Spain is now one of the biggest growers of fenugreek and its culinary influence is flecked across the southern parts of the country.

I soak the seeds briefly to soften which makes them easier to crush in a pestle and mortar. They have a natural affinity with tomatoes and when slow-cooked together over time produce a sublimely fresh tasting sauce.

The migas adds crunch to the dish, the cheese an extra layer of freshness and if you are feeling meaty some chorizo would make a wonderful bedfellow.

Serves 4

olive oil
2 large courgettes, cut in
    half lengthways
2 garlic cloves, crushed
5 sprigs of thyme
3 bay leaves
1 teaspoon fenugreek seeds,
    soaked in cold water for 20
    minutes and drained
1 small onion, finely chopped

500g vine-ripened
    tomatoes, quartered
2 teaspoons tomato purée
1 teaspoon caster sugar
1 slice day-old sourdough bread,
    ripped into small pieces
125g soft sheep's cheese or
    goat's cheese
sea salt and black pepper

Heat a large sauté pan over a medium heat and add a good glug of olive oil. When the oil is hot, place the courgettes cut side down in the pan and turn the heat down to low. Cook for 4 minutes to caramelise. Add the garlic, thyme, bay and soaked fenugreek seeds. Continue to cook cut side down for a further 3 minutes, then turn the courgettes over and cook until they are just tender. Using a slotted spoon, remove everything from the pan on to a plate and reserve.

Add the onion to the oil left in the pan and cook over a medium heat to soften. Add the tomatoes, tomato purée, sugar and seasoning and cook, stirring occasionally, for 25 minutes or until the tomatoes have broken down into a thick, chunky sauce. Check the seasoning again and remove from the heat.

While the tomato sauce is cooking, make the migas. Fry the bread pieces in hot olive oil until crisp and golden brown. Season and reserve.

Place the courgettes in the tomato sauce and reheat over a low heat. Sprinkle over the migas and serve with a pot of sheep's cheese on the side.

Watermelon and Salty Blue Cheese
with Toasted Walnuts and Moscatel Vinegar

The Moors introduced the watermelon to Spain towards the end of the 10th century. The fruit became wildly popular due to its sweet, refreshing flesh, and soon the word had spread throughout the countries of southern Europe.

Like many I love to eat watermelon on its own, chilled, when it's blazing hot, but I also love this combination of the sweet fruit's pairing with the salty blue cheese and the crunchy, salted walnuts.

Moscatel vinegar, or Muscat grape vinegar, is a delicious sweet vinegar with a gently sharp edge. A white balsamic would be a good alternative.

Serves 4–6

½ small, heavy watermelon (800g–1kg) with unblemished smooth, shiny skin
50ml moscatel vinegar or white balsamic
100g walnut halves

70ml walnut oil
a handful of herb fennel or dill fronds
150g salty blue cheese (such as Gorgonzola, Picos Blue, Roquefort)
sea salt and black pepper

Peel the melon half, removing all the white flesh under the skin. Dice the coloured flesh into 2cm pieces. Place in a bowl. Season and toss in the vinegar. Set aside.

Place a sauté pan over a medium heat. Break the walnut halves into pieces directly into the pan and toast for a few minutes, tossing, until they are fragrant and have started to release their oil. Season liberally with salt and mix into the watermelon.

Add the walnut oil and fennel fronds. and crumble in the blue cheese. Briefly mix together and serve. This is delicious on its own, with warm flatbreads, or as part of a mezze-style sharing meal.

Tomato Salad
with Radish, Green Chilli, Lemon and Coriander Seeds

This dish is all about the tomatoes. You can buy tomatoes all year round but so often they have little flavour, are desperately insipid and disappointingly watery. Heritage varieties have become popular and can have great depth of flavour and good texture.

The summer months in the UK see the sweeter variety of tomatoes arriving in the shops – plum vine, marmonde and cherry – but early tomatoes in April and May with flavour and sweetness can also be found, such as the varieties grown in the Isle of Wight.

I like to produce a selection of tomatoes in a salad with differing colours, shapes and textures and ranging in sweetness and acidity. Perhaps some quite sharp green tomatoes with a firm crunch to set alongside some super sweet vine-ripened cherry tomatoes.

Serves 4

500g mixed ripe but firm tomatoes
  in season
½ teaspoon ground sumac
juice of 1 lemon
1 tablespoon coriander seeds
12 breakfast radishes, leaves intact
  and washed

1 large fresh green chilli, deseeded
  and finely sliced
75ml extra virgin olive oil
50ml chardonnay or moscatel vinegar
sea salt and black pepper

Remove stalks and 'eyes' from the tomatoes, as necessary. Cut smaller tomatoes in half and slice any larger tomatoes into 1cm rounds with a serrated knife. Place the tomatoes in a bowl and season with the sumac and salt and pepper to taste. Squeeze over the lemon juice. Toss well, then leave to marinate for 10 minutes.

Meanwhile, put the coriander seeds into a small dry pan and toast them for 2–3 minutes or until fragrant. Immediately transfer them to the tomatoes. Cut each radish into quarters lengthways, with the leaves, and mix these into the tomatoes along with the chilli.

Whisk together the extra virgin olive oil and vinegar and stir this into the salad. Serve.

Pan-fried Asparagus
with Soft-boiled Egg and Romesco

British asparagus, one of the jewels in the British culinary crown, is ready in early spring, weather depending. The much-anticipated vegetable is harvested and delivered as quickly as possible before the stalks begin to toughen after picking as the natural sugars begin to turn starchy.

Romesco is one of my favourite sauces. The addition of nuts naturally thickens and adds texture. You can play about with varieties to suit your taste but almonds are a classic, and I like to add walnuts too for earthiness.

The recipe on page 288 will give you more than you need for the dish, so store in the fridge in a jar and use it with meats, grilled fish and all manner of vegetables. I prefer to use roasted peppers from a jar or tin for the sauce.

Serves 4 as a starter

4 medium free-range eggs
500g English asparagus
olive oil

30g unsalted butter
Romesco Sauce (see page 288), to serve
sea salt and black pepper

Soft-boil the eggs (4 minutes from boiling), then drain off the water and refresh the eggs under cold running water for 2 minutes until cold. Carefully peel the eggs and set aside.

Break the woody ends from the asparagus spears, then peel the stems from about halfway down. Set a large sauté pan over a medium heat and add a glug of olive oil and the butter. When the butter begins to foam, place the asparagus in the pan and season well. Cook for 3 minutes, turning the asparagus frequently. The butter will start to turn brown and the asparagus will become tender. Remove from the heat and transfer the asparagus to kitchen paper to drain.

Divide the asparagus among the plates and add a good dollop of romesco to each (romesco is always best served at room temperature). Cut the eggs in half lengthways, season and add to the plates.

Chilled Seasonal Greens
with Lemon, Chilli, Crispy Garlic and Cumin

I can't think of a better way to eat green vegetables in the summer than this simple and beautiful recipe. This uses an inspired culinary technique from southern Italy, usually reserved just for large leaf spinach, where the vegetables are cooked very briefly and then chilled at fridge temperature before dressing with the best olive oil, sea salt and plenty of lemon juice. Refreshing, zingy and delicious.

This method is a deceptively simple but genius Arabic concept used to create cold vegetable dishes dressed with sharp, mouth-puckering juice or vinegar and oil, and was developed out of the necessity to keep cool and refreshed in brutally hot temperatures.

I've introduced some Moorish flavours into the dressing – cumin, chilli and some crispy, slightly bitter garlic chips.

Serves 4

600g mixed seasonal greens (cavolo nero, kale, chard, turnip tops, sprouting broccoli – some texture and colour variety is good)
olive oil
3 garlic cloves, finely sliced
50ml extra virgin olive oil

1 teaspoon cumin seeds
2 red chillies, deseeded and finely sliced
grated zest and juice of 1 unwaxed lemon
sea salt and black pepper

Trim the greens as necessary, cutting off any hard stalks. Broccoli stalks should be cut into thin strips so they cook evenly. Bring a large pan of salted water to the boil and plunge in the greens. Cook for 2–3 minutes, ensuring there's still an *al dente* bite. Drain the vegetables in a colander and immediately refresh in a bowl of iced water. When fully cold drain again and gently squeeze excess water out of the vegetables. Keep in the fridge until needed.

Pour 1cm of olive oil into a small pan and heat. When very hot, carefully sprinkle in the garlic slices and fry them, stirring, until they are golden brown. Remove immediately with a slotted spoon and drain on kitchen paper. Season.

Warm the extra virgin olive oil in another small pan. Add the cumin seeds and set aside to infuse and cool for 5 minutes.

To serve, place the greens in a large bowl, along with the chillies, lemon zest and juice and seasoning. Pour over the cumin oil and toss everything together well. Taste to check the seasoning. Transfer the greens to a serving bowl, sprinkle over the garlic chips and serve.

Charcoal-grilled Green and Yellow Beans
with Sherry Vinegar and Bottarga

This is a lovely way to cook beans. The charring sets and intensifies the sweetness of the beans while the addition of sherry vinegar, olive oil and bottarga when still hot ensures the flavours develop wonderfully.

Bottarga is the Sicilian name for salted and air-dried mullet roe and is a wonderful and much prized salty-sweet delicacy. A good Italian deli should be able to source this for you.

Serves 4
as a starter or
part of a mezze

350g mixed green and yellow
  wax beans or French beans,
  ends trimmed
olive oil
75ml extra virgin olive oil

50ml aged sherry vinegar
1 teaspoon muscovado sugar
a piece of bottarga, about 20–30g
½ teaspoon ground sumac
sea salt and black pepper

If you are going to use a barbecue to grill the beans, then light the charcoal and let the coals turn to ashen grey – the optimum cooking temperature. If you are going to use a ridged grill pan, then heat it over a medium heat.

Bring a pan of salted water to the boil. Plunge in the beans and blanch for 2 minutes. Drain in a colander and immediately refresh in cold running water. Drain again and dry with a clean tea towel.

Toss the beans with some olive oil and seasoning, then lay them on the barbecue or grill pan and cook for 3 minutes, turning them frequently – you want to achieve a good char and smokiness. Transfer the beans to a bowl.

Whisk together the extra virgin olive oil, vinegar and sugar and pour over the beans. Season again. Grate over about 20g of the bottarga (or more if you like: it is quite strong). Toss through the beans, then divide among the plates. Sprinkle over the sumac and serve.

Tuna Tartare
with Fresh Apple, Cumin and Apple Vinegar

I first discovered this blissful combination of fresh tuna and apple at a beach restaurant on an island just off the coast of Sicily. Simply very rare tuna with mounds of shaved or diced apple and lemon juice piled on top. I loved the sweet, slightly sharp flavour of the apple set against the metallic, briny tuna.

Once back home I set out to create my version for a summer menu and this was the result. The hint of cumin works beautifully with the apple, adding a mild smokiness to the tartare.

It's essential you buy very fresh, red tuna for this dish and that the apple vinegar is of good quality, I use an excellent organic apple cider vinegar that is nicely balanced and not too sour.

Serves 4
as a starter

1 small Granny Smith or other crisp
    fresh apple
juice of ½ lemon
400g very fresh tuna (sushi grade
    is best)
½ teaspoon cumin seeds, lightly
    toasted and crushed

½ teaspoon runny honey
2 teaspoons apple vinegar or apple
    cider vinegar
2 teaspoons rapeseed oil
a small handful of coriander shoots
    or picked leaves, to garnish
sea salt and black pepper

Peel the apple and discard the core. Chop the apple into small dice and toss with a little lemon juice to prevent discolouration. Set aside.

Dice the tuna into 1cm pieces and place in a bowl. Add the crushed cumin seeds, a little squeeze of lemon and some seasoning.

Whisk together the honey, vinegar and rapeseed oil. Pour over the tuna and mix well. Leave to marinate for a couple of minutes.

Divide the tuna among chilled serving plates. Season the apple, toss with the coriander shoots and pile on top of the tuna. Serve.

Red Prawn Crudo
with Lemon, Rosemary and Sea Salt

Crudo is popular in the baking heat of Sicily where minimal preparation is very much the order of the day. Just caught shellfish and fish are eaten almost raw apart from a light, instant curing of salt and acid from citrus fruits. You could also add further flavours such as freshly chopped rosemary or toasted cumin seeds.

Be sure to use only spankingly fresh prawns – frozen and defrosted are fine as long as they are the very best quality.

Serves 4
as a starter

12 large, super fresh, raw red or tiger
    prawns, or langoustines
pared zest and juice of
    ½ unwaxed lemon

2 teaspoons picked rosemary leaves
Maldon sea salt

I like to leave the heads on the prawns, but remove them if you wish. Carefully peel off the shells and discard. Gently run a very sharp paring knife down the back of each prawn and remove the dark or grey intestinal vein. Rinse the prawns briefly in cold water, pat dry and place in a bowl.

Sprinkle some sea salt over the prawns followed by the lemon juice. Leave for 5 minutes to lightly cure.

Meanwhile, finely chop the rosemary and slice the lemon zest into strips.

Divide the prawns among the plates. Sprinkle with the rosemary and lemon zest and serve immediately.

Gazpacho
with Spiced Crab Toasts

It would be hard to find a Spanish dish with more recorded history than the gazpacho. Traceable back to Roman times, when soldiers on the march would carry stale bread, vinegar and garlic to make a quick soup when on the go, it wasn't until much later that the Arabs started flavouring this traditional mix with herbs, vegetables and nuts.

The word gazpacho is often used generically across Spain to describe a cold soup, whether it be an ajo blanco or a salmorejo, but the true gazpacho, a medium thick, piquant, chilled tomato soup, drinkable from a cup or glass, was first honed in Andalucía. The Moors married the technique with the local glut of tomatoes, pounding everything together to make this brilliantly refreshing, sharp soup.

There are as many variations on gazpacho as there are soups based on texture and flavourings not to mention the garnishes which can range from eggs and jamón, to all varieties of chopped vegetables and beyond – all have a place in the gazpacho pantheon. This is my version.

Serves 4–6

Gazpacho
1kg very ripe plum tomatoes
1 large red pepper, deseeded
½ cucumber, cut into chunks
1 large banana shallot, chopped
1 fresh red chilli, cut in
    half lengthways
2 garlic cloves, crushed
a handful of basil, leaves picked
70g day-old crusty bread, roughly torn
300ml fresh, good-quality
    tomato juice
50ml extra virgin olive oil, plus extra
    to drizzle

100ml moscatel vinegar or
    white balsamic
sea salt and black pepper

Crab toasts
olive oil
2 slices of sourdough bread, cut into
    6 pieces
200g white crab meat, picked over to
    remove any shell or cartilage
½ teaspoon ground cumin
lemon juice, to taste
1 small fresh red chilli, finely chopped
a handful of coriander leaves, chopped

First make the gazpacho. Quarter the tomatoes and pepper, and put all the ingredients in a bowl or other container along with 100ml of cold water and some seasoning. Cover and leave in the fridge for at least 4 hours, or overnight, to allow the flavour to develop.

Transfer the tomato mixture to a blender (you will need to do this in 2 batches) and blitz to a purée – the consistency should be that of a thick soup. Pour into a bowl. Check the seasoning. If the gazpacho is too thick you can add a splash of water. Return to the fridge to keep cool until ready to serve.

For the crab toasts, heat a sauté pan over a high heat, add some olive oil and fry the bread on both sides until golden brown and crisp. Transfer to kitchen paper to drain. Mix the crab with the cumin, lemon juice, chilli and coriander, and season to taste.

To serve, pour the gazpacho into chilled bowls and drizzle over some extra virgin olive oil. Top the bread slices with the crab mix and place in the gazpacho bowls.

Clams
with Garlic, Brown Butter and Hazelnut Picada

All the brown hues and seasonal nuttiness make this feel like an autumnal plate but it can and should be eaten all year round.

Originating in Moorish Spain, picada is a type of dual-purpose sauce using bread and nuts as the base. It is a wonderful vessel for herbs, spices and citrus zests and is also a natural thickener adding flavour and texture. It's great whisked into casseroles and stews near the end of cooking, but I love it in this dish when mixed with the caramelised butter, sherry and clam juices.

This recipe could also work really well with fresh mussels.

Serves 4

400g clams (venus or palourde), washed very well in cold running water and any broken clams discarded
2 garlic cloves, finely chopped
175ml dry sherry (fino)
3 sprigs of thyme
2 bay leaves
50g unsalted butter
juice of ½ lemon

Picada
a slice of white country bread, crusts removed and cut into chunks

70g peeled hazelnuts
1 teaspoon picked thyme leaves
½ teaspoon grated orange zest
a small handful of flat-leaf parsley
150ml brown butter (butter cooked over a medium heat until it turns a nut brown colour)
sea salt and black pepper

For the picada, put all the ingredients into a food processor and blitz to a paste. Season to taste.

Heat a large pan over a medium heat and add the clams, garlic, sherry, thyme and bay leaves. Cover the pan and shake it well (this helps the clams open), then leave to steam for 4 minutes. Check the clams are all opened; discard any unopened ones. Now add the butter and lemon juice and stir well.

Transfer the clams to serving dishes and pour over the cooking liquor. Spoon around the picada and serve.

Crispy Squid
with Chickpea Batter and Orange Alioli

Coated in a delicious light batter and then fried quickly in hot oil, this is one of my favourite ways to cook squid. The squid will remain tender and juicy with a light, crisp crunch from the batter. I like to use gram flour in the recipe which gives the dish a sweet, nutty undertone.

The orange alioli on page 282 will make more than you need for this recipe and is delicious with grilled and fried fish and roast chicken, so store in the fridge for use later (it will keep for up to a week).

Serves 4

160g chickpea flour (gram flour)
a pinch of baking powder
½ teaspoon fine salt
2 garlic cloves, finely chopped
½ teaspoon fennel seeds
1 teaspoon cumin seeds

vegetable oil, for deep-frying
250g prepared and cleaned fresh
    squid with tentacles, bodies opened
    out, scored and cut into chunks
Orange Alioli (see page 282)
sea salt

Sift the flour and baking powder into a bowl and add the fine salt and garlic. Gradually mix in enough cold water to form a thick batter. Put the fennel and cumin seeds in a mortar and roughly grind with the pestle. Add to the batter and mix in. Set the batter aside to rest for 15 minutes.

Meanwhile, heat the vegetable oil in a deep pan or deep-fat fryer to 180°C.

Add the squid chunks and tentacles to the batter, coating the pieces well. Deep-fry in batches until crisp and golden brown. Season with sea salt and serve with the orange alioli.

Steamed Mussels, Fennel and Cucumber Salad
with Coriander Seed and Lemon Vinaigrette

I enjoyed a similar salad to this while visiting the Aeolian islands off the north-east coast of Sicily, where razor clams were used as the star of the show. The food there is light, fresh, zesty and full of colour, with spices and almonds used in abundance in many of the islands' traditional recipes. Here, the accompanying cucumber and coriander salad is wonderfully vibrant and refreshing, taking me right back to my holidays.

Try to get large, plump mussels for this salad as the cooking process will inevitably shrink the mussels to some degree.

Serves 4

1.5kg very fresh, large, rope-grown mussels, beards removed and washed very well under cold running water
1 small fresh red chilli, split open and deseeded
a small glass of white wine
2 teaspoons coriander seeds

100ml extra virgin olive oil
juice of 1 small lemon
1 teaspoon caster sugar
1 small, firm bulb of fennel with fronds
½ cucumber
sea salt and black pepper

Check through the mussels and discard any that are open or don't look so good. Set a large pot over a high heat and get it quite hot, then throw in the mussels and add the chilli and wine. Cover the pot and steam the mussels for about 6 minutes or until they have all opened (discard any that haven't). Immediately drain the mussels in a colander set over a bowl to catch the cooking liquor. Discard the chilli.

Lightly toast the coriander seeds in a small dry pan until fragrant. Transfer to a bowl and pour over the olive oil and lemon juice. Add the sugar and seasoning and stir to mix. Add a tablespoon of the mussel cooking liquor and whisk well to combine. Set aside.

Cut the fennel bulb vertically in half. Cut out the core, then slice the fennel very thinly – use a mandoline for the best results. Shave strips/ribbons off the cucumber using a speed peeler until you reach the central seeded part (discard this). Put the fennel and cucumber into a bowl and season well.

Remove the mussels from their shells and mix them in with the fennel and cucumber. Pour in two-thirds of the lemon-coriander seed vinaigrette and toss through.

Present the salad in a bowl and the remaining dressing in a jug for those who want more. Serve with some warm crusty bread to mop up the juices.

Broad Bean, Tomato and Anchovy Salad
with Home-made Labneh

This is a mid-summer salad which depends upon using the freshest of ingredients for success, when bright green chalky broad beans are in abundance and tomatoes are at their sweetest. The Spanish tinned, salted Ortiz anchovies are among the best you can buy. They are plump, packed with flavour, not overly salty with just a little sweetness. Try to source Ortiz or a similar top-quality brand. Cheap, supermarket anchovies just won't cut the mustard.

   Though traditionally served with fresh, soft sheep or goat's cheese, I like to include a labneh instead. Labneh is essentially strained yoghurt and is a very popular Middle Eastern/Arabic preparation and, although not authentically Moorish, works brilliantly with this super salad.

Serves 4–6

100g podded fresh broad beans or
   thawed frozen broad beans
500g mixed ripe tomatoes in season
   (with a good colour selection)
extra virgin olive oil

aged sherry vinegar
Home-made Labneh (see page 52)
8 salted anchovies, chopped
sea salt and black pepper

If using fresh broad beans, blanch them in boiling salted water for 1 minute, then drain in a colander and refresh under cold running water. Drain well. Remove their grey 'jackets' to reveal the bright green beans. If you are using frozen beans (which I find to be of excellent quality), you only need to thaw before removing the 'jackets'.

Slice the tomatoes into 1cm rounds. Lay them on a large plate, season well and drizzle over extra virgin olive oil and a little sherry vinegar. Leave to marinate for 20 minutes.

To assemble the salad, spoon some labneh on to a serving plate and pile the tomato slices on top. Mix the broad beans with the anchovies, adding just a splash of olive oil and sherry vinegar to dress them, and spoon over the tomatoes. I've served this alongside my Mackerel and Salted Grapes (see page 94) and very delicious it was too.

Mackerel and Salted Grapes
with Cucumber, Yoghurt and Fennel

The cooling effects of yoghurt and cucumber are well known and often used in many world cuisines, whether in the raitas of India, a tzatziki in Greece or cacik in Turkey. The happy combination not only aides protection from the heat but also tempers spices and strong flavours and cuts through the fattiness of meat or fish.

This dish was inspired by a wonderful lunch I had in Córdoba in Andalucía on a baking hot July day. Pickled cucumbers were served with piping hot grilled mullets and a dollop of yoghurt on top. I've added some salted grapes for a sweet and salty accent and plumped for mackerel on the unashamedly selfish grounds that it is simply one of my favourites, but feel free to choose any meaty fish.

Try to get the small, firm, pickling cucumbers for this dish though a regular cucumber will do but you'll need to take out the watery centre.

Serves 4

4 very small cucumbers or
   1 medium cucumber
2 teaspoons caster sugar
½ teaspoon saffron threads
80ml white wine vinegar
16 green seedless grapes
16 black seedless grapes

olive oil
4 mackerel fillets, skin lightly
   scored with a sharp knife
100ml thick Greek yoghurt
a handful of herb fennel or dill
sea salt and black pepper

Preheat the oven to 120°C/100°C fan/Gas Mark ½.

Trim the small cucumbers, then peel in strips. If using a medium cucumber, trim and peel it in strips, then cut it in half lengthways and scoop out the watery centre. Cut each half across in half. Put the cucumbers in a bowl.

Put the sugar, saffron and vinegar in a pan with 90ml of cold water and bring to the boil. Remove from the heat and cool, then pour over the cucumbers. Cover the bowl and leave to pickle in the fridge for at least 1 hour.

Meanwhile cut the grapes in half lengthways. Place on a tray, drizzle over a little olive oil and sprinkle with sea salt. Place in the oven to dry out for 30 minutes – the grapes should have shrivelled slightly. Set aside to cool.

Heat a large non-stick sauté pan over a medium heat and add a glug of olive oil. Season the mackerel fillets. When the oil is hot, place the fish skin side down in the pan, carefully pressing the fish down to flatten them as they will bow. Cook for 4 minutes or until the skin is browned and crisp. Flip the fillets over and cook for a further 2 minutes or until the fish is just cooked through.

Spoon the yoghurt on to serving plates. Add the pickled cucumber, salted grapes and mackerel fillets. Sprinkle over the fennel and serve.

Calabrian-style Sea Bream
with Bergamot, Oregano and Nduja

Both bergamot and nduja are indigenous to Calabria in southern Italy. Bergamot, a type of highly perfumed orange, and nduja, a fiery pork-based pâté, couldn't be more different but work marvellously together in this fresh, spicy marinade for the meaty sea bream.

Nduja has become fashionable over recent years (in part due to its promotion from Calabria-born chef and mate of mine Franco Mazzezi) and has become fairly easy to obtain. Bergamot, on the other hand, is only available in specialist shops and when in season over the mid-winter months. A bitter orange variety would make for a good alternative.

Serves 4

85g nduja, skin removed
2 tablespoons extra virgin olive oil
2 tablespoons moscatel vinegar or
    white balsamic
1 large bergamot (or a bitter orange
    such as Seville)

4 large sea bream fillets, skinned and
    cut into 1cm slices
8 sprigs of oregano, leaves picked
sea salt and black pepper

Put the nduja in a saucepan and add 2 tablespoons of water. Slowly bring to the boil, mashing the nduja with a fork to create a 'sauce'-like consistency. Remove from the heat and whisk in the oil and vinegar. Set aside to cool.

Zest a third of the bergamot. Using a sharp knife peel away the rest of the skin and pith. Working over a bowl, cut the segments from the dividing membrane. Squeeze the membrane over the bowl to extract all the juice. Set the segments and zest aside.

Place the bream slices on a large plate or tray and pour over the bergamot juice followed by the nduja-vinegar sauce. Massage the fillets to ensure they are completely covered with the juice and nduja mixture. Leave in the fridge for at least 20 minutes to 'cure'.

About 10 minutes before serving, remove the fish from the fridge and divide among serving plates, or place on one platter to share. Add some of the marinade to each plate. Place the bergamot segments on top and sprinkle with the bergamot zest and oregano leaves. Serve.

Salt Hake Brandada
with Piquillo, Thyme and Orange Oil

This favourite is one of the most familiar dishes on the Andalucían tapas circuit. Smoky piquillo peppers stuffed with salted and whipped fish is a classic, but when doused in vibrant orange and thyme oil it's given a real hit of sunshine.

Hake has become my go-to white, meaty fish. Though criminally underused in the UK the fish-obsessed Spaniards have been championing it for decades. It has all the attributes of cod, though perhaps a little sweeter and a little less firm, and is one of the most sustainable fish on the planet.

Serves 4

350g hake fillet (skin on), pin-boned
100g sea salt
200ml full-cream milk
2 garlic cloves, each cut into 3
1 star anise
1 bay leaf
150ml light extra virgin olive oil
lemon juice
1 x 200g jar or can roasted, peeled
   whole piquillo peppers, drained
black pepper

Orange oil
500ml light extra virgin olive oil
pared zest of 2 oranges
a small handful of thyme, plus extra
   to garnish

First make the orange oil. Heat the oil in a saucepan until it is warm (don't boil). Add the zest and continue to heat gently for 10 minutes. Pour into a jar or other lidded container and add the thyme. Cover and leave to steep for at least 4 hours. This will make more orange oil than you need for this recipe but it can be used for dressing many things such as salads, vegetables and fish.

Place the hake in a bowl, pour over the salt and massage it into the fish. Leave to 'cure' for 3 hours in the fridge, turning once. Wash the hake under cold running water for a few minutes to rinse off the salt.

Pat the fish dry, then place in a saucepan with the milk, garlic, star anise and bay leaf. Bring to the boil, then simmer for 8 minutes. Remove from the heat and leave to cool before removing the fish and garlic and placing in a bowl (reserve the milk). Discard the fish skin. Mash the flesh and garlic together with a fork, adding some of the milk as you go to moisten (only a few splashes: you don't want the mix to be too wet). Slowly pour in the olive oil, stirring quickly as you go to emulsify the paste and oil to create the brandada. Season to taste with lemon juice and black pepper.

Stuff the brandada into the pepper cavities to fill completely. Chill the stuffed peppers in the fridge for 30 minutes. Serve them drizzled with the orange oil and sprinkled with fresh thyme leaves.

CHARCOAL, GRILLING & SMOKE

I love to cook over a live fire.

In 2014 I opened my restaurant Ember Yard where everything was cooked over wood or charcoal, Mediterranean style. The dishes were inspired by the techniques and flavours found in Spain and Italy – slow-cooked, spiced, smoky, meat, lots of fish, vegetables and fruit.

Take a trip through Sicily or Andalucía and you will see restaurants and homes all cooking this way, using the grill as an extension of the kitchen – at the most basic, a simple wood-fired grill built at the back of the building.

The Arabs refined the art of cooking over an open fire, bringing their knowledge along with their culinary wisdom on their conquest of southern Europe. Their inherent understanding of how to harness flavour and how best to cook fresh ingredients was inspiring and influential. Smoke was used as a flavouring, spices infused dishes as they cooked, while vegetables were laid on the dying embers of the fire to soften and take on delicious charred, smoky flavours.

When arriving in Europe the Moors looked to the local lean livestock for sustenance, which was duly slaughtered, rubbed and basted with herbs such as cinnamon, marjoram and cumin to install maximum taste and then cooked whole over a slow fire thus ensuring the meat didn't dry out.

Experience has taught us about the finer points of cooking with fire and which wood works best with which kind of produce. Oak is a great all-rounder but has a preference for the fatty meat flavours. Silver birch is light and fresh and works well with fish and vegetables. Cherry and apple wood are great with chicken and lighter, lean meats.

There's no better way to cook fresh fish than quickly over the grill, burnishing the skin so that it's charred and crispy, the flesh lightly cooked retaining its moist, juicy flavour.

Pinchos morunos typifies the Moorish legacy in Spain – a type of kebab that has developed over the years to become one of Andalucía's signature dishes. Originally the kebab would have been lamb but now you are just as likely to find it threaded with Ibérico pork, spiced with cumin, smoked paprika and black pepper and grilled quickly over a charcoal grill so that it caramelises on the outside while remaining pink and juicy within, finished with a sprinkling of good olive oil and lemon. (See pages 121–125 for my take on this classic.)

All the recipes in this chapter are at their best when cooked over charcoal or wood but will also be delicious if cooked using an oven grill or griddle – just be prepared to open the kitchen windows to let the smoke out.

Whole Roast Cauliflower
with Caramelised Onions and Rose Harissa

Cauliflowers are incredibly versatile and they really take to roast and grilling – rather like a piece of meat – largely due to their density and how compact the florets are. Don't discard the cauliflower leaves; they are incredibly delicious when roasted and help the cooking process of this dish by gently steaming the cauliflower from beneath.

Cauliflower dishes are popular in Sicily where they roast the florets and toss through pasta dishes and gratins, perhaps with spices such as saffron and sweetness from raisins. This particular dish has more of a nod to the Middle East than Sicily, but the spirit and inspiration is there.

Do try to get the sublime rose harissa, if not a regular harissa will do nicely.

Serves 4

1 large, leafy cauliflower
½ teaspoon coriander seeds
½ teaspoon cumin seeds
½ teaspoon fennel seeds
½ teaspoon sweet smoked paprika
¼ teaspoon dried chilli flakes
½ teaspoon ground cinnamon

olive oil
3 garlic cloves, finely chopped
2 onions, finely sliced
100ml thick Greek yoghurt
50ml rose harissa
sea salt and black pepper

Preheat the oven to 170°C/150°C fan/Gas Mark 3½.

Trim the very end of the base of the cauliflower to flatten it, so the cauliflower can stand up straight on its own. Place the cauliflower on a roasting tray and spread out the cauliflower leaves at the base.

Put all the spices into a pestle and mortar or spice grinder and grind to a powder.

Liberally drizzle olive oil over the cauliflower and leaves, then sprinkle with the spices and garlic. Season well. Rub the cauliflower with your hands to massage in the spices. Place in the oven and roast for 25 minutes.

Drizzle more oil over the cauliflower and turn down the heat to 140°C/120°C fan/Gas Mark 1. Roast for a further 1 hour or until the cauliflower is beautifully browned and very tender.

Meanwhile, heat some oil in a medium saucepan, add the onions and cook over a medium heat for 25 minutes or until they are a deep golden brown.

Serve the cauliflower hot, cutting into 4 wedges at the table. Dollop some yoghurt, fried onions and rose harissa on to each wedge.

Stuffed Aubergines
with Almonds, Parsley and Preserved Lemon

The aubergine is a wonderful vegetable much in need of an exotic climate to flourish to its full potential. And as Spain has just such a climate and terrain the Moors eagerly introduced this most richly satisfying of vegetables to the Mediterranean early in the Middle Ages – it has flourished there ever since. Ibn al Awwam, in his treatise on agriculture written in the 12th century, describes exactly how to grow the perfect aubergine in the ideal climate and his guidance, knowingly or otherwise, is followed to this day.

As a cook, it is hard not to love the aubergine but it does demand the right cooking techniques to bring out the best in it. A bland and watery aubergine is a crime against your time and the vegetable itself. Deep-frying in a light batter is a lovely technique that can produce wonderful results though I prefer charring and smoking the skin over an open flame, softening the delicious flesh within.

Preserved lemon can be easily obtained from delis and larger supermarkets.

Serves 4

4 small, firm aubergines with bright, unblemished skin	70g blanched almonds
olive oil	50g pitted green olives (drained weight)
4 garlic cloves, finely chopped	40ml red wine vinegar
1 teaspoon fenugreek seeds, crushed	50ml extra virgin olive oil
70g day-old sourdough bread, torn into small pieces	60g preserved lemon (drained weight), finely chopped
a handful of flat-leaf parsley	sea salt and black pepper

Preheat the oven to 190°C/170°C fan/Gas Mark 5, or set up and light your barbecue. Prick the aubergines lightly with a fork. If you will be baking the aubergines in the oven, hold them, one at a time, on a long-handled fork over a direct flame on the hob to blister and char the skin all over. If using a barbecue place the aubergines over the hot coals and cook, turning with tongs, until the skin is blistered and charred. Set the aubergines aside.

Heat a glug of olive oil in a sauté pan over a low heat, add the garlic and fry until softened and very lightly browned. Add the fenugreek and bread and continue to cook for 3 minutes or until the bread has browned and the fenugreek is fragrant. Place the bread-garlic mix in a food processor along with the parsley, almonds, olives, red wine vinegar and extra virgin olive oil. Pulse-blitz for 1 minute to form a rough paste. Transfer to a bowl. Season this stuffing and stir in the preserved lemon.

Slit the aubergines open from stalk to base, cutting only about two-thirds of the way through so they are still intact. Fill the cavities with the stuffing. Drizzle over some olive oil and season. Wrap each aubergine in foil, then either place on a baking tray in the oven or back on the barbecue (to the side of the coals and with the lid closed). Cook for about 25 minutes or until the aubergine flesh is very soft.

Remove the aubergines and leave to rest for 10 minutes before opening the foil parcels and serving (leaving in the foil for a rustic touch). Serve with labneh (see page 52) or yoghurt.

Left: *Whole Roast Cauliflower with Caramelised Onions and Rose Harissa (see page 102)*
Right: *Stuffed Aubergines with Almonds, Parsley and Preserved Lemon (page 103)*

Charcoal-grilled Peaches
with Goat's Cheese, Chestnut Honey and Toasted Almonds

I love to cook stone fruits over the barbecue – the sugars slowly caramelise intensifying the fruits' sweetness while lightly singeing and smoking the edges. This is where the beauty of live-fire cooking comes into its own.

I use a Spanish goat's cheese for this recipe but any soft, creamy cheese will do nicely – it's important that the cheese contrasts and cools the sweet smoky peaches. Chestnut honey adds a deep, nutty-caramel flavour to the proceedings.

Serves 4

60g blanched almonds, cut in half
extra virgin olive oil, for drizzling
4 firm white or yellow peaches, cut in
    half and stone removed
8 sprigs of thyme

120g soft, fresh goat's cheese
2 tablespoons chestnut honey
    or a quality runny honey
sea salt

Prepare and light a charcoal fire in a barbecue – the coals should burn down to an ashen grey before cooking. Alternatively, heat a ridged grill pan over maximum heat on the hob.

Toast the almonds in a small dry pan until lightly golden. Season with sea salt and drizzle over some olive oil, then set aside.

Dab the cut side of the peach halves with kitchen paper to soak up excess moisture, then drizzle with a little oil. Place the peaches cut side down on the barbecue or grill pan and cook for 4–5 minutes or until caramelised and lightly singed at the edges. The juices will drip on to the hot coals and create a little smoke that will flavour the peaches.

Turn the peaches over and lay a sprig of thyme on each cut side. Continue to cook for 2–3 minutes to soften the peaches on the other side.

Divide the grilled peaches and goat's cheese among 4 plates or bowls. Drizzle over the honey and scatter the almonds on top. Serve as a starter or a cheese course.

Violet Artichokes Cooked in Embers
with Pine Nut, Cumin and Milk Sauce

The food markets of Sicily are awash with artichokes in the summer months. The artichoke is taken very seriously in Sicily and is one of the season's highlights.

The favourite way to cook these is over charcoal, nestled in the embers of a fire or barbecue. Drive through Sicily during the summer season and you'll see plumes of smoke bellowing out all along your route. And the smoke is the key to this dish, working deliciously with the bitterness of the artichokes.

I prefer the smaller, more tender artichokes for this recipe – the larger ones can still be tough even after a couple of hours in the coals.

Serves 4

100ml extra virgin olive oil
a small handful of flat-leaf parsley,
   finely chopped
4 garlic cloves, finely chopped
12 young, fresh artichokes,
   stems trimmed

juice of 1 lemon
1 quantity Pine Nut, Cumin and
   Milk Sauce (see page 287)
sea salt

Prepare and light a charcoal fire in a barbecue. When the coals have turned ashen grey, spread them out evenly.

Whisk together the oil, parsley and garlic along with a pinch of salt. Toss the artichokes through this mix, then place them in the barbecue, nestling them into the embers (use long-handled tongs). There will be a lot of smoke initially but don't be alarmed – this will flavour the artichokes. When the smoke dies down, leave the artichokes to cook for 1½–2 hours, turning them occasionally to ensure even cooking.

Remove the artichokes from the barbecue and cut them into quarters. Place on a serving dish. Squeeze over the lemon juice, sprinkle with sea salt and pour over any remaining olive oil-parsley mix. Serve with the pine nut, cumin and milk sauce.

Note: The artichokes can also be cooked on a baking tray in the oven at 170°C/150°C fan/ Gas Mark 3½ for the same time. You won't get the smokiness but they will be delicious all the same.

Olive Oil-roasted Potatoes
with Green Peppers, Chilli and Green Olives

This is my spin on the Andalucían classic 'patatas al o pobre' meaning 'poor man's potatoes'; essentially potatoes with whatever you have knocking about in the fridge!

I wanted to refine this staple, as I love potatoes so much, adding a decent olive oil, the right potatoes and some fresh, green punchy flavours to make this dish excellent. Serve with anything you like or with a bowl of alioli (see page 282).

Serves 4
as a side dish

750g King Edward or red Rooster
    potatoes, peeled
about 130ml extra virgin olive oil
    (I use a good Spanish Arbequina)
3 garlic cloves (unpeeled), crushed
2 small green peppers, deseeded and
    cut into fine slices

1 large fresh green chilli, deseeded
    and finely chopped
50g pitted green olives, finely chopped
a handful of coriander, roughly
    chopped including stalks
sea salt and black pepper

Cut the potatoes into bite-size chunks, then place in a pan and cover with cold water. Season and bring to the boil. Simmer until the potatoes are three-quarters cooked – still a little raw in the middle. Drain very well in a colander and shake the potatoes to release their steam. Spread out the potatoes on a tray to cool down (I often do this outside on the garden table, covering the potatoes with a clean tea towel).

Preheat the oven to its maximum heat. Put an oven tray, large enough to fit the potatoes on one layer, into the oven to heat up.

Pour the olive oil on to the hot tray, then carefully place the potatoes in the oil along with the garlic. Season with plenty of salt and pepper. Place the tray back in the oven and roast the potatoes for 20 minutes – they will have begun to crisp and brown and can now be turned over.

Turn the oven down to 200°C/180°C fan/Gas Mark 6 and return the tray to the oven. Roast for 10 minutes, then shake the tray well. Add the green peppers and chilli and mix with the potatoes. Place back in the oven to roast for about 10 minutes. By now the potatoes should be crisp and evenly browned and the peppers and chilli should have softened. Roast for a few minutes longer if the potatoes need to be more brown.

Remove the potatoes from the oven and immediately sprinkle over the olives and coriander. Stir through. Using a slotted spoon transfer the potatoes to a serving bowl and serve immediately.

Grilled Squids
with Heritage Tomato, Orange and Cardamom Salad

This dish was inspired by a recipe from the brilliant *Honey and Co.* cookbook. I've known Sarit and Itamr for years and used to take my team to their restaurant for inspirational staff meetings or my wife Nykeeta and I would go for lovely, relaxed dinners.

Their food is Israeli influenced, where they are both from originally, and of course the overlaps into Moorish cuisine are profound.

Their dish used prawns cooked down with tomatoes, oranges and infused with cardamom. This is more salad-y and the squids are grilled for a smoky contrast to the fresh, cool tomatoes and orange.

Serves 4

4 prepared and cleaned squid
    with tentacles
80ml groundnut oil
2 cardamom pods, crushed
400g heritage tomatoes in season
    (a mix of colour and texture), cut
    into 1cm slices
2 banana shallots, finely sliced
    into rings
1 teaspoon picked thyme leaves

2 medium, sweet oranges
80ml orange juice (you should get
    this from the sweet oranges when
    segmenting; if not, top up with
    extra juice)
20ml runny honey
2 tablespoons moscatel or
    chardonnay vinegar
olive oil
sea salt and black pepper

Place the prepared squid in a sink and rinse well, inside and out, under cold running water. Slit the bodies open to lie flat and score with a sharp knife, then dry well on kitchen paper – they must be very dry before grilling, otherwise they'll release water and boil. Cut the tentacles in half.

Heat the groundnut oil in a small saucepan with the cardamom until hot. Remove from the heat and set aside to infuse.

Prepare a charcoal fire in the barbecue or heat a ridged grill pan.

Put the tomatoes, shallots, thyme and some seasoning into a bowl and mix well. Peel the oranges, removing all the white pith, then segment them, working over a bowl to catch the juice. Add the segments and 80ml of orange juice to the tomatoes.

Strain the cardamom-infused oil into a small bowl. Whisk in the honey and vinegar. Reserve 1 tablespoon of this dressing, and pour the remainder over the tomatoes. Toss gently. Leave the tomatoes to marinate at room temperature.

Drizzle some olive oil over the squid and season well, then cook them over the hot coals or on the grill pan for 3 minutes – without disturbing them so they caramelise well. Turn them over and cook for 3 minutes on the other side. Remove from the heat, cut each squid into 4 or 5 pieces and spoon over the reserved dressing. Divide the tomato and orange salad among plates and top with the squid.

Fresh Mackerel Kebabs
with Garden Onions and Tahini

Mackerel, along with other oily fish like sardines, are perfect for grilling. They self-lubricate and baste while cooking over a high heats and their skins get marvellously crisped and blistered while the flesh stays juicy and succulent.

It's imperative you use spanking fresh fish – not only does it taste much better but it will be firmer and more rigid which enables easier skewering and managing on the grill.

The tahini rub gives extra flavour and nutty caramelisation.

Serves 4

4 large mackerel fillets, pin-boned and
    each cut into 8 pieces
1 teaspoon picked thyme leaves
2 garlic cloves, finely chopped
1 fresh red chilli, deseeded and
    finely chopped
1 teaspoon sesame seeds
olive oil

150g thick Greek yoghurt
150g tahini
juice of ½ lemon
8 thick garden onions or large spring
    onions, ends trimmed and each cut
    into 4 pieces
sea salt and black pepper

Place the mackerel pieces in a bowl with the thyme, garlic, chilli and sesame seeds. Season well and drizzle over some olive oil. Toss to mix. Leave to marinate in the fridge for 30 minutes.

Meanwhile, whisk the yoghurt with the tahini and 25ml of cold water. Season with salt, pepper and lemon juice. The sauce consistency should be thick yet brushable. If it is too thick, add a little more water.

Prepare a medium charcoal fire in the barbecue, or heat a ridged grill pan or overhead grill to moderate.

Thread the mackerel pieces and onions alternately on to 8 long metal skewers so you have 4 pieces of each on each skewer. Brush some of the tahini-yoghurt sauce on the kebabs and place them on the barbecue or grill pan (or on the tray under the overhead grill, if using). Cook for 3 minutes. Brush with more sauce, then turn the kebabs and cook for a further 3 minutes. Remove from the heat and rest. The mackerel flesh should still be a touch pink inside and charred on the outside along with the onions.

Serve the kebabs with the remaining tahini sauce. I also like to eat this with my Chilled Seasonal Greens (see page 76) and Olive Oil-roasted Potatoes (see page 110).

Smoky Sardines
with Crushed Fennel Seeds, Slow-cooked Onions and Sumac

Oily fish such as sardines and mackerel are perfect cooked quickly over a charcoal grill or griddle as their natural oiliness lubricates the flesh during the fast cooking process.

Fennel features twice in this recipe, fresh, cooked long and slow with onions into a sweet-sour Sicilian-style stew, and then in its highly aniseed-y form, crushed and sprinkled onto the sardines before grilling, creating an extra crunch and an aromatic flavour.

Serves 4
as a starter or mezze

2 medium bulbs of fennel
olive oil
2 medium onions, thinly sliced
2 garlic cloves, thinly sliced
2 teaspoons brown sugar
50ml moscatel vinegar
3 sprigs of thyme
2 bay leaves

juice of ½ lemon
8 fresh sardines, gutted, scaled
   and cleaned
2 tablespoons fennel seeds, crushed
   in a pestle and mortar
½ teaspoon ground sumac
sea salt and black pepper

Remove the fronds from the fennel and reserve. Cut out the core, then slice the fennel bulbs very finely lengthways, preferably using a mandoline.

Heat a medium saucepan over a high heat and add a glug of olive oil followed by the fennel, onions and garlic. Cook for 5 minutes, stirring, then turn down the heat to low and add the sugar, vinegar, thyme and bay leaves. Cover and cook for 50 minutes or until the vegetables are nicely caramelised and meltingly tender. Season with salt, pepper and a little of the lemon juice, then set aside.

Prepare a charcoal fire in the barbecue or heat a ridged grill pan to a medium-high heat. If you are using the barbecue, wait until the coals are an ashen grey.

Rub the sardines with olive oil and season. Sprinkle the crushed fennel seeds over the sardines and press into the fish skin. Lay the sardines on the barbecue or grill pan and cook for 2 minutes on each side or until the skin and fennel seeds are nicely charred and the fish is just cooked through.

Remove the sardines from the heat and squeeze a little lemon juice over them. Sprinkle with the sumac. Rest for 3 minutes before serving alongside the fennel-onion stew, topped with the reserved fennel fronds. This would also be delicious served with the Charcoal-grilled Green and Yellow Beans (see page 78).

Whole Brill
with Peppers, Tomato and Pomegranate

I first had fish cooked this way in San Sebastian, in the Basque country in northern Spain. The fish was actually turbot and had been cooked for about 10 minutes over a hot (but not too hot) grill filled with glowing silver birch logs. It was the most exquisite of things – cooking fish this way on the bone keeps it incredibly moist and flavoursome but more importantly the bones release their natural gelatine into the fish, making it incredibly unctuous. This southern Spanish-Moorish version uses the cheaper, but no less delicious, brill and comes with smoky Mediterranean peppers and tomatoes and a simple pomegranate dressing.

Investing in a barbecue fish clamp will make this much easier and looks very impressive. You can of course do this in the oven too, albeit without the smokiness.

Serves 4–5

2 red peppers, deseeded and quartered
4 large, vine-ripened plum tomatoes,
    cut in half
olive oil
75ml quality red wine vinegar
100ml extra virgin olive oil
75ml pomegranate molasses

1 whole brill, about 3kg, gutted
juice of ½ lemon
seeds from ½ large pomegranate
a small handful of oregano or
    marjoram, leaves picked
sea salt and black pepper

Prepare and light a charcoal fire in a kettle-type barbecue to optimum heat, using good charcoal and a soaked oak log for smokiness. Let the coals burn down until they turn ashen grey. The internal temperature of the barbecue should be about 200°C. (Alternatively, preheat the oven to 180°C/160°C fan/Gas Mark 4.)

Toss the peppers and tomatoes in a little olive oil and seasoning, then spread on an oven tray. Place on the barbecue grill and close the lid (or place in the oven). Cook for about 25 minutes or until charred, smoky and softened. Remove from the barbecue (or oven).

Whisk together the vinegar, extra virgin olive oil and pomegranate molasses in a bowl. Drizzle some of this vinaigrette over the peppers and tomatoes, then set aside.

Season the brill and rub with a little olive oil. Place in a fish clamp and cook on the barbecue for 7–8 minutes or until the fish has started to caramelise. Turn over and cook for a further 5–6 minutes. (If cooking in the oven, place the fish on an oven tray lined with baking parchment and roast for 25 minutes or until the flesh is translucent and cooked through.)

Remove from the barbecue (or oven) to a tray. Squeeze over the lemon juice, then cover the brill with foil and leave to rest in a warm spot for 10 minutes. Meanwhile, pour the fish resting juices into the remaining vinaigrette along with the pomegranate seeds. Whisk together. Transfer to a jug or bowl for pouring.

Serve the fish, peppers and tomatoes on a platter, sprinkled with the oregano, and pass around the sauce.

Spiced Venison Pinchos
with Pancetta and Membrillo

Another version of the pinchitos (the name used in the autonomous regions of southern Spain, Andalucía and Extremadura) that have derived from the Moorish occupation – essentially skewered meat kebabs that are usually associated with North Africa and the Middle East.

These are smaller, tapas-sized skewers designed for eating with a vino tinto or sherry, and cooked over charcoal until slightly blackened, smoky and pink inside. The pancetta element here helps keep the super lean venison juicy through the cooking process, and the quince adds a lovely sweet-sour glaze.

I serve these alongside the classic pinchos murunos (see page 125) straight from the barbecue, absolutely delicious!

Serves 4
as a mezze

300g boneless venison haunch, cut
    into 2cm cubes
6 sprigs of thyme
2 garlic cloves, finely chopped
10g caster sugar
1 teaspoon cumin seeds, crushed
1 teaspoon ground cinnamon
½ teaspoon coriander seeds, crushed

100g thinly sliced pancetta
sea salt and black pepper

Quince glaze
75g membrillo (quince paste)
20ml cabernet sauvignon or
    moscatel vinegar

Put the venison into a bowl with the thyme, garlic, sugar, spices and seasoning. Leave to marinate for at least 1 hour before cooking.

You need 8 long skewers, either metal or wooden. If using wooden skewers, soak them in cold water for an hour.

Wrap a piece of sliced pancetta around each venison cube. Thread them on to the skewers.

To make the glaze, gently melt the quince in a small pan with the vinegar and 1 tablespoon of water over a low heat until liquid.

Prepare a charcoal fire in a barbecue and burn until the coals are ashen grey, or heat a ridged grill pan over a medium heat. Brush the kebabs with the quince glaze, then place on the barbecue, or in the grill pan, and cook on all sides to caramelise – the venison should still be pink inside. Keep brushing with the glaze as you go. Rest for 3 minutes before serving.

I like to serve these with my Pine Nut, Cumin and Milk Sauce (see page 287).

Left: Messina-style Veal Skewers (see page 124)
Middle: Spiced Venison Pinchos with Pancetta and Membrillo (see page 121)
Right: Ibérico Pork Pinchos with Smoked Paprika (see page 125)

Messina-style Veal Skewers

Byzantine Messina fell to Moorish invaders around 882. In fact, it was a fairly quick process, as the natives opened their city gates and allowed the Moors to occupy without too much bloodshed and avoided a massacre as seen in cities such as Taormia. The culinary influence the Arabs left on this city and the rest of Sicily is staggering, and still so very evident.

This dish uses a Sicilian favourite of lean veal rump that's marinated in a paste of green olives, anchovy, preserved lemon, garlic and fresh green herbs and then grilled on skewers, kebab-style. It's not unusual to see North African-style street grilling in the towns of Sicily during the summer months, and you could quite easily think you were in Morocco.

I only use rose veal that means the calves have had a longer life and time outside, resulting in tastier, better meat. Lamb or pork are good alternatives.

Makes 6 kebabs

650g boneless rose veal rump, cut into 2cm cubes
100ml light extra virgin olive oil
2 fresh green chillies, deseeded
120g pitted green olives
4 salted anchovies
50g preserved lemon peel

1 teaspoon coriander seeds, toasted and lightly crushed
2 teaspoons ground almonds
a small handful of flat-leaf parsley leaves
a small handful of mint leaves
sea salt and black pepper

Place the veal in a large mixing bowl. Season well and drizzle over 50ml of the extra virgin olive oil.

Put the remaining ingredients in a blender along with the rest of the oil. Pulse-blitz until you have a rough paste. Season well.

Spoon the paste over the veal and massage it well into the meat – make sure all the pieces are fully coated. Cover the bowl and leave to marinate in the fridge for at least 4 hours.

Prepare a hot charcoal fire in the barbecue or preheat an overhead grill.

Thread the veal pieces on to metal skewers (15cm long), dividing them equally. Season the kebabs. Suspend the skewers over the barbecue grid so they are not directly touching the bars. If using an overhead grill, balance the ends of the skewers on the edges of the grill pan so they are suspended. This way the meat will cook and the marinade will caramelise without sticking. Cook, turning regularly, for 8–9 minutes or until the veal is well browned but still pink inside.

Rest in a warm spot for 5 minutes before serving with my home-made Chickpea and Spelt Flatbread (see page 30) and Charcoal-grilled Green and Yellow Beans (see page 78).

Ibérico Pork Pinchos
with Smoked Paprika

This is a classic Andalucían tapa – a little meat skewer that is marinated in cumin, smoked paprika and lemon and then grilled over charcoal until charred and smoky. Clearly a resemblance to the North African kebab, and during the Muslim rule in Andalucía and Extremadura these would have been made with lamb. The pinchito is now more likely to be made with Ibérico pork (the favourite meat of southern Spain) but the spice and cooking techniques live on.

During the summer months the streets of southern Spanish towns are filled with sweet smoke from pinchito parties – rowdy, wine-fuelled affairs where everyone brings along plates of their 'own recipe' skewers to be grilled at the designated party host's house ... and there's always a bit of rivalry on the best recipe.

Makes 8 skewers

500g boneless Ibérico pork loin (or boneless lamb shoulder or a quality rare-breed pork loin), trimmed of most of the fat
4 teaspoons sweet smoked paprika
2 teaspoons cumin seeds, toasted

4 garlic cloves, finely chopped
300ml extra virgin olive oil
100ml cabernet sauvignon or red wine vinegar
juice of ½ lemon
sea salt and black pepper

Soak 8 wooden skewers (12cm long) in cold water for 1 hour. Dice the pork (or lamb) into about 3cm cubes. Thread on to the skewers – there should be about 4 pieces on each skewer. Place the skewers on a shallow tray.

Put the paprika, toasted cumin seeds, garlic, olive oil and vinegar into a bowl. Whisk together very well, then pour evenly over the pork. Turn the skewers to ensure they are all covered with the marinade. Leave to marinate in the fridge for about 2 hours. During this time, turn the pork skewers once.

Remove the pork skewers from the fridge and scrape off the excess marinade (reserve the marinade).

Prepare a charcoal fire in a barbecue or heat a ridged grill pan to a maximum heat. Season the pork, then place on the barbecue or grill pan. Cook for 2 minutes on one side or until caramelised, then turn on to the other side and cook for 2–3 minutes. Turn down the heat and cook for a further 2 minutes (or a further 4 minutes for regular pork).

Remove the skewers from the grill and leave to rest in a warm spot for 2–3 minutes. Meanwhile, put the reserved marinade in a small pan and bring to the boil. Spoon some of the marinade over the pinchos and squeeze over the lemon juice. The pinchos should be deeply caramelised and slightly charred with a juicy interior. The wooden skewers will be charred too, but don't worry about this – it adds an authentic presentation.

Blackened Ibérico Pork Presa
with Jamón and PX Sherry Butter

Ibérico pigs or Pata Negra are known as the king of pigs, an ancient breed native to the Iberian peninsula. The meat is truly unique, more akin to wild boar or even wagyu beef. The meat is red and has deep, rich marbling, which stems from their free-roaming lifestyle in the Dehesa and diet of rich, nutty acorns.

The cured version, jamón Ibérico, can be found on most tapas bar counters throughout Spain, sliced very thinly onto plates and served with a chilled glass of fino sherry, equally as delicious but very different. Ibérico products are now widely available, and the brilliant UK-based retailer Brindisa is leading the way with the best Spanish products.

This dish, with its pork and alcohol, clearly isn't a direct descendant from the Moorish occupation! However, for me it typifies how the two cultures have intertwined harmoniously – the spices with the pork and the cooking technique are very much of Arabic origin.

Serves 4

175g unsalted butter, at
  room temperature
2 tablespoons Pedro Ximinez
  (PX) sherry
25g jamón Ibérico (or serrano or
  Parma ham), finely diced
4 x 200g steaks of Ibérico pork
  presa (or beef rib-eye steaks)

1 teaspoon hot smoked paprika
1 teaspoon cumin seeds
1 teaspoon coriander seeds
2 tablespoons runny honey
olive oil
juice of ½ lemon
sea salt and black pepper

Place the butter in a bowl and whisk in the PX sherry and diced ham. Season well and reserve in a cool spot.

Place the pork steaks on a tray and season lightly. Crush the spices together in a pestle and mortar, then sprinkle over the pork, massaging them into the meat as you go. Drizzle over the honey and massage this into the meat too. Leave the pork to marinate for at least 1 hour or up to 6 hours.

Prepare a fire in the barbecue, or heat a ridged grill pan over medium/hot heat. Drizzle a little oil over the pork, then place over the hot coals or on the grill pan. Cook for 3–4 minutes on each side – the exterior will naturally blacken and caramelise to a crust, while the inside should be pink (the meat of Ibérico pigs is red and it is perfectly safe to eat it pink or even rare). Rest the meat for a few minutes in a warm spot.

Squeeze the lemon juice over the pork, then slice the steaks. Serve with a good spoon of the jamón butter on the side, and with my Caramelised Chicory (see page 182), if desired.

Smoky Charcoal-grilled Beef Rump
with Cooked Grape Must and Thyme

Grape must is freshly pressed grape juice, including the pips and skins, and is the first stage in the process of wine making before the fermenting happens. The juice then gets cooked down to make syrup that resembles a thick, aged balsamic but with much fresher notes. It's sold usually as saba or mosto cotto.

Because of its high sugar content and consistency it's brilliant for adding to a braise, sauces or even desserts, rather like a pomegranate molasses, and it also works brilliantly as a marinade and glaze. I recommended a barbecue for this dish as the real smokiness you get from a real charcoal and wood fire contrasts incredibly with the sweet, sticky, caramel-like must.

Serves 4

a well-aged boneless beef rump joint, about 1kg, with a good layer of fat (a thick piece is better for cooking on the barbecue)
3 garlic cloves, crushed and finely chopped

small handful of picked thyme leaves (stalks reserved)
500ml saba (see above), plus extra for final glazing
olive oil
sea salt and black pepper

Place the beef rump in a bowl. Season well and rub with the garlic and half the thyme leaves. Pour over the saba and massage well into the meat. Pour in enough water to submerge the beef. Cover, place in the fridge and leave to marinate for 8 hours, turning once or twice.

Remove the beef but reserve the marinade. Leave the meat at room temperature for 30 minutes before cooking.

Prepare a charcoal fire in the barbecue or set a large ridged grill pan on medium heat. If you are using a barbecue, you can throw the thyme stalks on to the hot coals (or wood) as you cook the beef, for an extra flavour boost.

Season the beef again and drizzle over a little oil, then place on the medium hot barbecue or grill pan. Cook for 4 minutes on one side to caramelise. Turn over and continue cooking to brown the other side. Take a pastry brush and lightly apply some of the marinade to the meat every time it is turned.

When all sides of the beef are caramelised (a thick piece of meat will need to be browned on 4 sides), move it to a cooler spot on the barbecue, or reduce the heat under the grill pan. Continue cooking but without too much further colouring, basting when you turn the meat, until the beef registers an internal temperature of 63°C on a probe thermometer (medium rare). This will take about 25 minutes in total. Cook for 5 minutes longer for medium or 10 minutes more for medium to well done. Leave the beef to rest in a warm spot for 30 minutes.

Brush liberally with extra saba and sprinkle over the remaining thyme. Serve sliced thickly with the resting juices poured over. My Salmoriglio sauce (see page 288) and Broad Bean, Tomato and Anchovy Salad (see page 92) go well with this delicious beef.

Charcoal-grilled Lamb Chops
with Fresh Peas and a Hot Cumin and Mint Vinaigrette

There's nothing like the smell of lamb chops cooked over charcoal – they seem to be made for it with the tasty fat lightly charring and crisping, the outside flesh caramelising and then the juicy pink inside. Absolute heaven. Here I've paired the chops with a simple but really interesting dressing I sampled in Sicily, although there the vinaigrette came with chalky broad beans and fresh fennel fronds instead of the peas and mint. Both versions are delicious.

I usually say that with grilling you can achieve the same result indoors as out, and it's mostly true, however for this I really think its worth wheeling out the barbecue and lighting some charcoal. I like to serve this with my Stuffed Aubergines (see page 103).

Serves 4

180g podded fresh English peas
(or frozen garden peas)
8 new-season's lamb chops, trimmed
of excess fat
olive oil
juice of ½ lemon
150ml extra virgin olive oil

100ml white balsamic vinegar
1 teaspoon cumin seeds,
lightly crushed
3 garlic cloves, finely sliced
mint leaves, to garnish
sea salt and black pepper

Prepare a charcoal fire in your barbecue or heat a ridged grill pan.

Bring a pan of salted water to the boil and blanch the peas until just tender. Drain and refresh in iced water. Drain again and set aside.

Season the chops well and rub with olive oil. Place on the barbecue or grill pan and cook on one side for 4 minutes. There should be a good caramelisation when the chops are turned over, along with a slight charring along the fat. Cook on the other side for 3 minutes for medium rare – the meat should have a good spring when pressed. Remove the chops from the heat to a wire rack set over a tray and squeeze over the lemon juice. Leave to rest in a warm spot for 5–7 minutes.

Meanwhile, whisk together the extra virgin olive oil and vinegar in a small saucepan. Season well and add the cumin and garlic. Heat until the garlic just starts to fizz. Add the peas and remove from the heat. Pour in the lamb resting juices that have dripped into the tray and check the seasoning.

To serve, divide some of the peas, along with some of the vinaigrette, among 4 serving plates. Place 2 lamb chops on top of each pile of peas, then spoon over the remainder of the peas and vinaigrette. Finish each plate with a sprinkle of mint leaves.

Wood-baked Moorish Chicken Pie

This is the Andalucía-Moorish version of the complex Moroccan pastilla although not as sweet and less time consuming. The pastela moruna can be found in many of the bakeries in Granada and history dictates that this pie was created by Moorish aristocracy in the Alhambra Palace and then kept alive by local nuns cooking in the convents.

Traditionally the pastela is baked in a wood oven and the pastry absorbs some of the smokiness during cooking, adding another layer of flavour and giving the pie its distinct golden hue.

I don't bother making a fresh pastry for this recipe, as there's some excellent all-butter puff pastry available in the supermarkets. Do feel free to make your own if you like.

Serves 6–8

6 free-range chicken legs,
    skin removed
2 onions, finely chopped
1 tablespoon sweet smoked paprika
½ teaspoon ground cumin
¼ teaspoon ground ginger
½ teaspoon ground cinnamon
¼ teaspoon cayenne pepper
olive oil
200g plum tomatoes, roughly chopped

85g raisins
500ml dark chicken stock (home-
    made or ready-made fresh)
plain flour, for dusting
2 puff pastry sheets, 200g each
30g pine nuts
35g flaked almonds
1 egg yolk beaten with a splash of milk
icing sugar, for dusting
sea salt and black pepper

Preheat the oven to 180°C/160°C fan/Gas Mark 4.

Season the chicken and place in a large flameproof roasting tin along with the chopped onion, spices and a good drizzle of olive oil. Place in the oven and cook, turning the legs once or twice, for 40 minutes or until the chicken is cooked through and the juices run clear.

Remove the chicken from the oven and cool, then pick the meat from the legs in chunks. Discard the bones. Put the chicken meat back in the tray with the spices and onion and add the tomatoes, raisins and stock. Bring to a simmer and cook for about 45 minutes, or until the liquid has reduced and thickened. Set this filling aside to cool before stuffing the pie.

Lightly flour a work surface. Using a floured rolling pin, roll out one sheet of puff pastry to a roughly 30 x 40cm rectangle. Transfer it to an oiled 30 x 40cm baking tin/sheet. Roll out the remaining sheet of puff pastry to a rectangle that is slightly smaller than the first.

Spread the filling evenly over the pastry on the baking sheet, leaving about 3cm bare along each of the 4 edges. Sprinkle the pine nuts and almonds evenly on top. Cover the filling with the second pastry rectangle. Fold the edges of the bottom crust up over the edges of the top and crimp them decoratively. Brush the top of the pie with the egg wash. Using a sharp knife, make slits all over the top crust to allow steam to escape.

Prepare and light a charcoal fire in a kettle-type barbecue to optimum heat. Add a soaked oak log to the side of the coals. Move the coals and wood to the side of the barbecue so you have an indirect heat zone to create a steady, light smoke. Place the pie on the barbecue grill to the side of the coals (the indirect heat zone) and close the lid. The vent of the barbecue should be half closed. The internal temperature of the barbecue should be around 180°C. Cook the pie for 40 minutes or until golden brown and piping hot inside.

Alternatively, you can bake the pie in the oven at 180°C/160°C fan/Gas Mark 4 for 40 minutes.

Remove the pie from the barbecue or oven and dust with icing sugar before serving.

Pheasant and Harissa

This dish has a real North African feel to it. The smell of caramelising harissa paste cooked over the flames of a barbecue sends you off to Marrakech or Fez, but you are as likely to find this in the markets and streets of Cádiz, Córdoba and Granada.

Marinating the pheasant in harissa not only adds its fiery, smoky delicious flavour but helps to moisten and tenderise the meat. You can do the same with partridge, pigeon or even chicken.

Serves 4

4 oven-ready pheasants
1 quantity Harissa (see page 283) or about 200ml quality ready-made harissa

grated zest and juice of
   1 unwaxed lemon
olive oil
sea salt and black pepper

You need 8 long skewers, either wooden or metal. If wooden, soak in cold water for 1 hour before use.

Spatchcock the birds or ask your butcher to do this for you. To spatchcock each pheasant, lay it breast side down on a chopping board and press down firmly to flatten it. Using poultry shears or sturdy kitchen scissors, cut through the backbone and ribs and remove them. Insert 2 skewers diagonally on opposite sides to hold the bird flat in shape during cooking. Score the legs with a sharp knife 2 or 3 times to speed up the cooking process.

Place the pheasants, skin side up, on a tray. Spoon over the harissa, add the lemon zest and rub into the pheasants, ensuring they are evenly coated. Cover and leave in the fridge for about 2 hours. Before cooking, remove from the fridge so the pheasants can come up to room temperature.

Prepare and light a charcoal fire in a barbecue – the coals need to turn an ashen grey before cooking. Alternatively, heat a ridged grill pan over a medium heat.

Season the pheasants and drizzle with a little oil. Place them on the hot barbecue or grill pan (cook in batches, if necessary) and cook for 3 minutes on the breast side to caramelise. Turn the birds over and either move them to a cooler spot on the barbecue or turn the heat down under the grill pan. Cook slowly for 8 minutes, turning them over once. The birds should still be a little pink inside and nicely caramelised and crisp on the outside.

Remove the pheasants from the barbecue or pan. Squeeze over the lemon juice and season again, then leave the birds to rest in a warm spot for 10 minutes before serving. I often serve this with my Home-made Goat's Milk Labneh with Fresh Peas, Broad Beans, Almonds and Mint (see page 52).

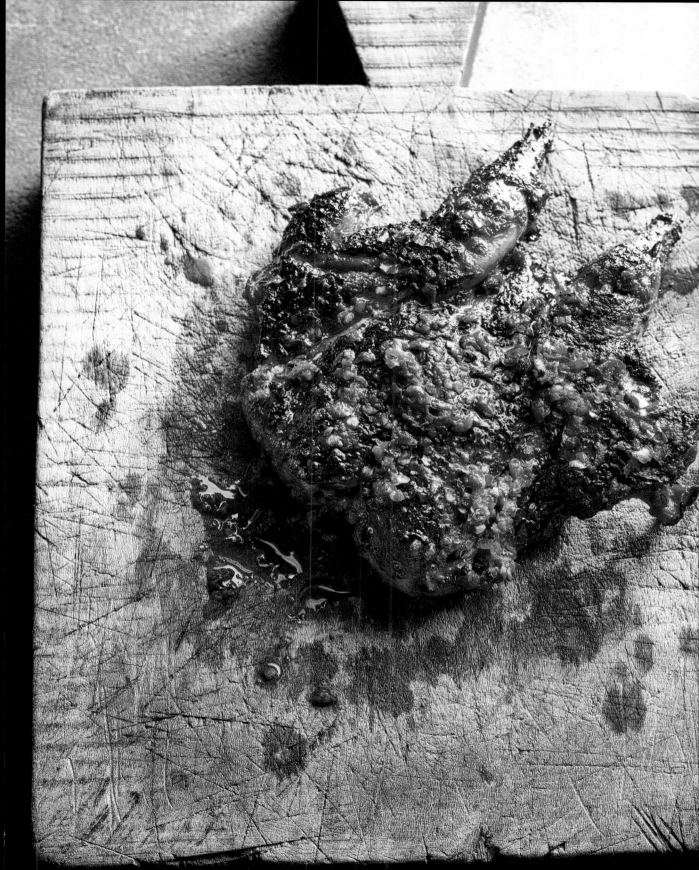

Chicken with Apricots and Sumac

An unusual Sicilian-Moorish inspired dish where chicken is slowly cooked in a wood oven along with apricots, almonds, olives and sumac.

I use a mix of dried and fresh apricots for this recipe – the fresh apricots break down into the chicken juices creating a wonderful sweet-sour sauce while the dried apricots hold their shape and provide a lovely texture.

Serves 4

4 free-range chicken legs, thigh and
    drumstick separated
olive oil
1 onion, finely chopped
1 garlic clove, chopped
4 sprigs of thyme
1 teaspoon ground ginger
50g dried apricots, roughly chopped

4 fresh ripe apricots, cut in half and
    stone removed
700ml dark chicken stock (home-
    made or ready-made fresh)
1 teaspoon ground sumac
70g blanched almonds,
    roughly chopped
sea salt and black pepper

Prepare and light a charcoal fire in a kettle-style barbecue. Shuffle the hot coals to one side and place a small soaked log at the edge of the coals to smoke lightly. The internal temperature of the barbecue should be 180–190°C. Alternatively, preheat the oven to 180°C/160°C fan/Gas Mark 4.

Meanwhile, heat a large flameproof casserole over a medium heat on the hob. Season the chicken pieces. Add a glug of olive oil to the pot and, when hot, brown the chicken pieces all over until golden. Remove the chicken from the pot.

Add more oil to the pot and cook the onion with the garlic and thyme for 3 minutes or until softened. Stir in the ginger and cook for a further 2 minutes. Place the chicken pieces back in the pot with the onions and add the dried and fresh apricots. Pour over the stock (this will only make a shallow depth in the pot, leaving the top of the chicken pieces uncovered so they can take on the smokiness in the barbecue).

Transfer the casserole to the barbecue, placing it on the side opposite where the coals are, and close the barbecue lid. Alternatively, cover the casserole and place in the oven. Cook for 1½ hours or until the chicken is cooked through and starting to come away from the bones, and the sauce is thick and rich. During the cooking time, stir a couple of times to prevent sticking.

Remove the casserole from the barbecue or oven and leave to rest for a few minutes before spooning off any excess fat and checking the seasoning. Sprinkle over the sumac and stir in the almonds, then serve.

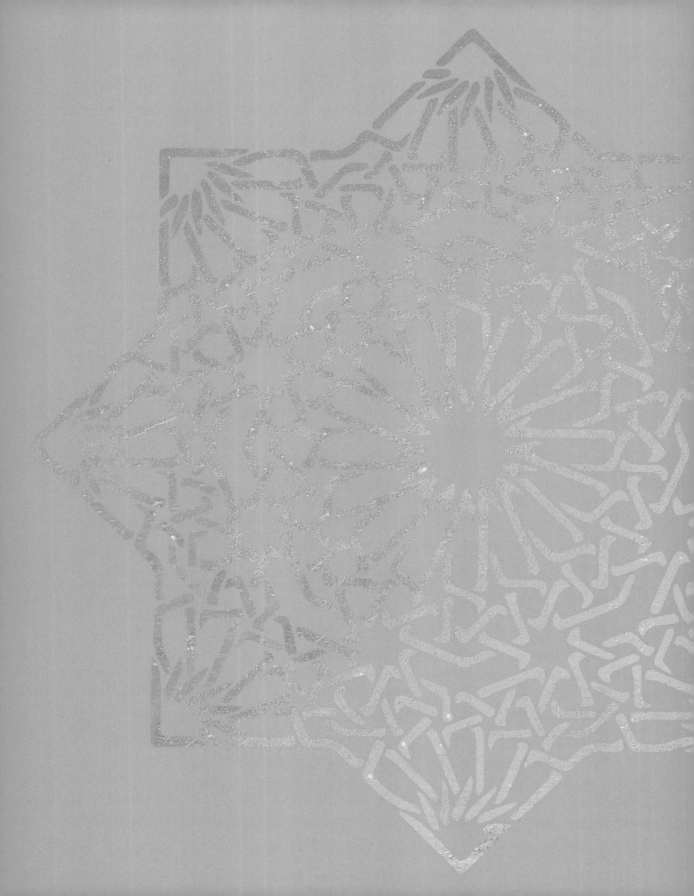

SLOW-COOKED

A carefully prepared slow-cooked dish is one of life's great culinary pleasures. Slow-cooked dishes require a degree of loving attention in their preparation and judicious care in their cooking in order to reach their perfect best. The depth of flavour resulting from slow-cooking is often a happy marriage of marinating, salting, braising and reducing. Slow-cooking concentrates and harnesses flavour and through the addition of spices, herbs, stocks and elements of sweetness can create a dish of wonder.

The Moors of North Africa introduced spicing and complexity into slow-cooking of which the tagine was the precursor. The introduction of fruits alongside meat by the Moors was a stroke of minor genius adding so much more than simple sweetness to the dish.

In this chapter I've included some familiar dishes, such as the popular Braised Oxtail with Chorizo, Red Wine and Sofrito (see page 165), alongside my own Moorish-inspired creations, such as tasty Pot-roasted Quails with Lemon Leaves, White Beans and Pomegranate (see page 176).

There are also vegetable dishes – Roasted Beetroots and Carrots with Toasted Cumin and Sheep's Cheese (see page 142).

Allow some time for these dishes, perhaps a weekend project when there's less time to rush and you can let the aromas flood around you. I find this type of cooking wonderfully therapeutic and restorative and would recommend it to anyone in need of serious de-stressing.

Roasted Beetroots and Carrots
with Toasted Cumin and Sheep's Cheese

A wonderful thing happens to beets and carrots when you cook them this way, slowly caramelising in their own natural sugars with the addition of salt and spices, concentrating the flavours to intensity.

The pungent, curry-like notes of black cumin seeds are a brilliant foil for the sweetness of the roots. All that's needed to finish is a salty sheep's cheese sprinkled over the dish while still warm – a good-quality feta will do the trick but if you can find an Andalucían raw milk sheep's cheese, such as Queso des los Pedroches, it will add a greater complexity. Check out Spanish delis such as Brindisa or Foods from Spain.

Serves 4

300g small beetroots
300g small carrots
30g black cumin seeds, lightly crushed
    with a pestle and mortar

400g rock salt
100g salty sheep's cheese (see above)
50ml extra virgin olive oil
25ml red wine vinegar

Preheat the oven to 170°C/150°C fan/Gas Mark 3½.

Trim the leaves and stalks from the beetroots and carrots (wash the leaves well and reserve for a salad). Rinse the beetroots and carrots and drain very well before spreading them on an oven tray.

Mix the cumin seeds with the salt. Pour the salt mix over the roots, ensuring they are fully covered. Place in the oven and roast for 1 hour to 1 hour 20 minutes or until the roots are very tender – check this by inserting the tip of a small sharp knife: it should glide in as if it were butter. Remove from the oven and cool for 10 minutes before excavating the roots.

Peel the skin off the beetroots with a blunt knife, then cut them in half. (Leave the carrots whole.)

To serve, arrange the beetroots and carrots in a serving dish. Crumble the cheese over the vegetables and drizzle over the oil and vinegar. Make a simple salad with the leaves from the roots to serve alongside.

Slow-cooked Squid
with Tomatoes, Olives and Preserved Lemon

Squid is normally associated with fast cooking, grilling or frying, but this recipe requires the squid to be slow-cooked in a bright and sunny tomato and olive sauce until rich and tender. The Moorish influence is apparent in the inclusion of aromatic fennel seeds and bay and the sour salty tang of preserved lemon.

Salting and preserving lemons was a method used by the Moors during the brief lemon harvest to ensure lemons were available year round.

This southern Italian-style recipe is excellent with cuttlefish or even octopus in place of the squid.

Serves 4

600g vine-ripened plum tomatoes
extra virgin olive oil
1 onion, chopped
2 garlic cloves, chopped
a handful of flat-leaf parsley,
   leaves picked and chopped
   (stalks reserved)
2 bay leaves
1 fresh red chilli, chopped with seeds

1 teaspoon fennel seeds, crushed
2 teaspoons tomato purée
125ml white wine
800g prepared and cleaned squid, cut
   into chunks, plus tentacles
100g pitted green olives
100g preserved lemon, peel
   only, chopped
sea salt and black pepper

Preheat the oven to 160°C/140°C fan/Gas Mark 3.

Trim the 'eyes' out of the tomatoes, then blanch in a pan of boiling water for a minute until the skins start to peel off. Drain and leave to cool for a few minutes before discarding the skins. Roughly chop the flesh.

Heat a large flameproof casserole or ovenproof pan over a low-medium heat and add a glug of extra virgin olive oil. When hot, cook the onion and garlic gently for a few minutes to soften, without colouring. Add the parsley stalks, bay leaves, chilli, fennel seeds and tomato purée. Cook for 5 minutes, stirring as you go, then add the wine. Boil to reduce by half.

Add the chopped tomatoes and bring to a simmer. Stir in the squid and season well with salt and pepper. Put the lid on the casserole or pan and transfer to the oven. Cook for 1 hour. Add the olives and continue cooking, uncovered, for 30 minutes. When the stew is ready, the sauce will be thick and rich and the squid tender.

Remove from the oven and leave to rest for 20 minutes before stirring in the chopped parsley and preserved lemon. Serve on toasted slices of my home-made Sobrassada and Cornmeal Bread (see page 34) or ciabatta grilled with olive oil.

Slow-cooked Fish and Shellfish Stew
with Saffron and Star Anise

An intensely flavoured and aromatic fish stew inspired by Sicily. The colours alone are inviting and rich, helped by the addition of grated butternut squash (which also adds a sweetness) and the golden hue of saffron. I'd as happily eat this on a hot summer's day imagining myself in Palermo, as on a cold winter's evening sat in my kitchen by the fire at home. It's both warming and vibrant in equal measures and is a real favourite of mine.

Feel free to use seafood of your choice but remember it is quick to cook so just put it in during the last few minutes of cooking.

Serves 4

olive oil
¼ butternut squash, peeled and grated
1 large celery stick, diced
3 shallots, diced
1 large carrot, diced
2 star anise
1 cinnamon stick
a pinch of saffron threads
½ teaspoon coriander seeds, crushed
1 tablespoon tomato purée
75ml brandy
200ml white wine
1.5 litres fish stock (home-made or ready-made fresh)

400g vine-ripened tomatoes, chopped
150g fresh clams, well washed
150g fresh rope-grown mussels (the smaller the better), washed and beards removed
8 large, raw tiger or king prawns
500g skinless cod fillet (or fillet of other firm white-fleshed fish), diced
150 prepared and cleaned baby squid with tentacles, roughly chopped
juice of ½ lemon
1 tablespoon chopped flat-leaf parsley
sea salt and black pepper

Heat a large saucepan over a high heat and add a glug of olive oil followed by the vegetables, spices and tomato purée. Cook, stirring frequently, for 10 minutes or until the vegetables have browned and started to soften. Pour in the brandy and carefully set it alight. When the flames die down, add the wine and bring to the boil. Reduce for a few minutes before adding the stock and tomatoes. Turn the heat down to low and simmer gently for 1 hour or until rich and thickened, stirring occasionally.

Season to taste and add the clams, mussels and prawns. Cook for 5 minutes, then add the cod and squid. Cook for a further 2 minutes. Squeeze in some lemon juice and add the parsley. Remove from the heat and leave the stew to rest for a few minutes before dividing the seafood among bowls and spooning over the rich sauce.

Serve with warm focaccia (see Pane Cuzanto, page 27–28) spread with Saffron Alioli (see page 282).

Sicilian-style Seafood Cous Cous

Trapani is on Sicily's wild western coast and looks out to Tunisia. The Arab influence here is very strong. Cous cous is a staple part of the diet and the local name for the dish is cuscusu.

The Moors first produced the dish in its simplest form in the city of Marsala and it is really an early form of pasta – pasta is made from durum wheat flour whereas semolina are the grains left from the flour milling process and more granular in texture, and this is made into cous cous.

Cuscusu is taken very seriously on the west coast with specific bowls and utensils used for the preparation. There's even an annual cous cous festival that sees enthusiasts come from far and wide to showcase their recipes. Cous cous itself is great for stews as it absorbs all the broth's natural flavours. A long resting time is essential for a truly sublime result.

This seafood recipe is a hearty affair, ideal for a hungry Sicilian fisherman with plenty of fish to hand, or even for a hungry family of four!

Serves 5–6

400g mussels, washed and
   beards removed
6 large, raw king or tiger prawns
250g cous cous, rinsed in cold running
   water for a few minutes
olive oil a good pinch of dried
   chilli flakes
juice of ½ lemon
2 sea bream fillets, each cut into
   2 pieces
200g skinless cod fillet, cut
   into chunks
150g prepared cleaned squid with
   tentacles, roughly chopped

Broth
1 litre fish stock (home-made or ready-
   made fresh)
1 onion, chopped

1 carrot, chopped
1 celery stick, chopped
3 garlic cloves, crushed
3 bay leaves
a few sprigs of thyme
½ teaspoon saffron threads

Tomato sauce
1 onion, finely chopped
2 garlic cloves, finely chopped
50g ground almonds
1 teaspoon ground cumin
1 tablespoon tomato purée
300g ripe plum tomatoes, cored
   and chopped
a small bunch of curly parsley,
   roughly chopped
sea salt and black pepper

First make the broth. Pour the stock into a large saucepan and add the remaining ingredients. Bring to the boil, then simmer for 5 minutes. Add the mussels and prawns to the broth. Cover the pan and cook for a further 8 minutes or until the mussels have opened and the prawns are cooked through.

Remove from the heat and leave for 15 minutes before straining the broth through a sieve into another pan; set the broth aside. Pick the mussels and prawns out of the vegetables in the sieve, then discard the vegetables. Reserve the mussels (still in shell) and prawns.

...continued on page 150

Put the cous cous into a bowl, season and add a glug of olive oil and the chilli flakes. Stir with a fork to moisten the cous cous with the oil, separating the grains as you go.
Bring the strained broth back to the boil, then pour around 250ml over the cous cous (the cous cous should be covered with the broth plus a third more). Stir again with the fork. Cover the bowl with clingfilm so it is completely sealed, then set aside to steam and soak for 20 minutes. Stir again with the fork, separating the grains. Cover and steam for a further 25 minutes, then stir once more to separate the grains. Check the seasoning and add the lemon juice. Leave, covered, in a warm spot for at least 1 hour before serving.

While the cous cous is soaking make the tomato sauce. Put a good glug of olive oil in a large sauté pan set over a medium heat. Add the onion, garlic, ground almonds and cumin and cook, stirring, for a few minutes to soften without colouring. Stir in the tomato paste and cook for a further 2–3 minutes. Add the tomatoes and mix in, then cook, stirring occasionally, for 20 minutes or until the tomatoes have broken down into a sauce consistency. Season with salt and pepper.

Nestle the bream, cod and squid in the tomato sauce. Turn the heat to low, partly cover the pan and simmer gently for about 20 minutes or until the fish is cooked through and the sauce reduced.

Remove the lid and nestle the prawns and mussels among the fish. Sprinkle over the parsley. Cover again and cook gently for 10 minutes to finish reducing the sauce and warm through the prawns and mussels. Remove from the heat and leave to rest for 20 minutes, still covered.

Check the seasoning of the tomato sauce, then divide the seafood among serving bowls. Stir through the cous cous with a fork and check the seasoning. Serve with the seafood. A good fresh, sharp salad is all you need with this tasty, robust dish.

Octopus and Smoked Paprika
with Black Beans and Rice (Christians and Moors)

One of the many annual ceremonies celebrated in Granada is the 'Christians and Moors', which marks the time when the Moors were driven back to North Africa. The black beans represent the Moors and the rice the Christians! The dish is served all through the day with each restaurant and street vendor adding his or her own slant to the dish. My take is an addition of tender, smoked paprika-rubbed octopus.

The only rule you need to follow when cooking octopus is to buy frozen: defrost it slowly and then slow-cook for an hour or so. The freezing/defrosting process naturally tenderises the meat making it easy to cook. If you can only get hold of fresh octopus then freeze it and defrost yourself.

And in the spirit of inclusivity this dish now represents Christians, Moors and cephalopods.

Serves 4–6

Octopus
1 small frozen and thawed octopus, about 1.5kg
1 onion, peeled
1 carrot, washed
5 bay leaves
8 black peppercorns
1 star anise
juice of ½ lemon
olive oil
1 teaspoon sweet smoked paprika

Rice and beans
olive oil
1 large onion, finely diced

4 garlic cloves, chopped
120g unsmoked back bacon, diced (optional)
3 bay leaves
2 teaspoons ground cumin
300g long-grain rice, rinsed under cold water to remove the starch
1 x 400g can black beans, drained and rinsed
juice of ½ lemon
sea salt and black pepper

Put the octopus into a medium saucepan and cover with cold water by 2.5cm. Add the onion, carrot, bay leaves, peppercorns, star anise and lemon juice. Slowly bring to the boil, skimming off any scum that rises to the surface, then turn down to a simmer. Leave to cook for 1–1½ hours or until the octopus is very tender – the tip of a small sharp knife inserted into the thickest part of the octopus should glide in like butter. Remove from the heat.

Lift out the octopus on to a tray and set aside to cool. Strain the octopus cooking liquor – you'll need 750ml for the rice and beans (if there isn't enough, top up the liquor with water).

When the octopus is fully cooled, remove and discard the head, then separate the tentacles. Drizzle with oil. Sprinkle over the paprika and massage into the tentacles. Set aside.

...continued on page 152

For the rice and beans, heat a large flameproof casserole or a large saucepan over a medium heat, add a glug of olive oil and sweat the onions and garlic for a few minutes to soften without colour. Add the bacon (if using), the bay leaves and cumin and cook for a further 3 minutes. Stir in the rice, adding more olive oil if necessary to lubricate. Season well, then add 250ml of the reserved octopus cooking liquor. Cook slowly until the rice has soaked it all up. Continue cooking, adding the remaining octopus liquor a bit at a time so the rice can absorb it, for about 15 minutes or until the rice is soft and tender. Add the beans and stir in, then cook for a further 2 minutes. Remove from the heat and leave to rest, covered, for 2 minutes.

Slice the octopus tentacles into 2cm chunks and stir through the rice and beans. Season to taste and add some lemon juice. Serve immediately.

Whole Cinnamon-spiced Chicken and Pilaf

The elements of this dish are very simple, just roast chicken, some spice and some rice. But the technique of cooking everything together in the same pot amplifies all the flavours and creates the most delicious, sticky, lemony, unctuous cinnamon-spiced pilaf.

A good amount of credit for this recipe goes to Claire Thompson who wrote the brilliant *5 O'Clock Apron* cookbook. Her cinnamon chicken recipe is one of our family's favourites. Needless to say a great chicken will give you a great dish, so invest in the best you can.

Serves 4

1 free-range or organic chicken,
    1.8–2kg
6 sprigs of thyme
1 lemon, cut in half
olive oil
2 teaspoons ground cinnamon
½ teaspoon ground cumin
1 teaspoon ground coriander
1 onion, finely chopped

3 garlic cloves, finely chopped
1 cinnamon stick
3 bay leaves
350g basmati rice, rinsed well with
    cold water, then soaked in cold
    water for 30 minutes
a handful of flat-leaf parsley leaves,
    roughly chopped
sea salt and black pepper

Preheat the oven to 180°C/160°C fan/Gas Mark 4. You need a large, lidded ovenproof pan or flameproof casserole for this recipe, large enough to cook the chicken and rice together.

Stuff the chicken cavity with the thyme, a lemon half and seasoning. Heat the pan or casserole over a medium heat and add a good glug of olive oil. Brown the chicken all over, seasoning as you go, then sprinkle over the ground cinnamon, cumin and coriander. Transfer to the oven and roast for 30 minutes to further brown and cook the chicken.

Remove the pan or pot from the oven (leave the oven on) and lift the chicken on to a plate. Put the pan or pot back over a medium heat on the hob and add a little more oil. Add the onion with the garlic, cinnamon stick and bay leaves and cook in the oily juices until softened.

Drain the rice very well, then add to the pan. Stir well to coat with the juices and season. Pour over a glass of water. Place the chicken on the rice and press down, then put the lid on the pan or pot. Return to the oven and cook for 1 hour 20 minutes or until the chicken is cooked through and the juices run clear.

Remove from the oven and leave, covered, to rest for 20 minutes. The rice under the chicken will be tender and delicious from all the chicken juices and fat.

Lift the chicken on to a chopping board. Remove the legs and breasts and cut each in half. Stir the chopped parsley and juice of the other lemon half into the rice. Spoon it on to serving plates, top with the chicken and serve.

Slow-cooked Lamb Shoulder
with Butter Beans, Moorish Spices and Buttermilk

Lamb shoulder can be cooked as you might a cook a leg by quickly caramelising the outside and then giving it a quick roast until just pink. You'll find it toothsome but delicious.

However, my preferred way is to slow-cook, allowing the fat and flesh to melt into one another creating a lip-sticking, unctuous meat full of intensity. The herbs, spices and aromats here work their magic in the marinade and then through the cooking process.

As with all these types of things a generous resting time elevates everything.

Serves 5–6

4 garlic cloves, finely chopped
4 salted anchovies, chopped
4 teaspoons cumin seeds
2 teaspoons sweet smoked paprika
2 teaspoons ground cinnamon
grated zest of 1 orange
1 x 1.1kg boned shoulder of
 lamb, butterflied
olive oil
1 large onion, cut into quarters

2 carrots, cut in half
3 sprigs of thyme
3 sprigs of rosemary
3 bay leaves
300ml red wine
200ml pomegranate molasses
1 x 400g can butter beans, drained
 and rinsed
200ml buttermilk
sea salt and black pepper

Put the garlic, anchovies, spices and orange zest in a mortar and roughly grind down with a pestle. Place the lamb in a bowl. Season and rub with oil, then rub the ground spice mix all over. Leave the lamb to marinate in the fridge for at least 2 hours and up to 6.

Roll up the lamb and tie in three spots to hold it together (or use 3 elastic butcher's ties).

Preheat the oven to 150°C/130°C fan/Gas Mark 2.

Set a deep flameproof casserole over a medium heat on the hob. Put the lamb in the pot and brown on all sides; remove from the pot. Add the onion and carrots and cook for a few minutes to brown. Return the lamb to the pot, placing it on the vegetables along with the thyme, bay and rosemary. Cover the casserole and transfer to the oven to cook for 2½ hours or until the lamb is tender.

Take the casserole out of the oven and set aside, still covered, to cool for 30–40 minutes.

Remove the lamb and vegetables from the casserole and set aside. Carefully remove the fat from the cooking juices in the pot. Add the wine and pomegranate molasses to the juices, place the casserole on the hob and bring to the boil. Reduce until you achieve a sauce consistency.

Place the lamb and vegetables back in the pot to warm through along with the beans. Simmer for 2 minutes. Serve in the casserole, at the table family style, with the buttermilk on the side to spoon over each portion.

Andalucían Pork Ribs
with *Almonds and Coriander*

Ribs, like many of the cheaper, tougher cuts of meat, require some work to bring out the best in them, but the results are always rewarding and, as in this recipe, often stunning. Andalucíans love ribs. Lamb ribs are popular too and would have been the obvious choice for the Moors, who would have cooked them over a charcoal fire until crisp and charred.

The ribs in this recipe are delicious! The quince glaze is one of the best that I've ever used for ribs. It has a perfectly balanced sweet and sour flavour while the cooking liquor retains all the natural flavour and body from the bones, and can be used as a base for soups or as a delicious broth for cooking pulses.

This is one of my favourite summer dishes for when I'm cooking over fire. The ribs are equally as good straight from a hot griddle. Serve with some chips cooked in olive oil.

Serves 4

1.2kg pork ribs (ideally cut from the
    belly of a well-reared heritage pig)
150g sea salt
½ bulb of garlic, separated into cloves
a few sprigs of thyme
4 bay leaves
3 star anise

2 cloves
170g membrillo (quince paste)
25g coriander seeds
10g hot smoked paprika
50g flaked almonds, lightly toasted
a small handful of coriander,
    leaves picked

Rinse the ribs under cold running water, then cut into 3–4 rib pieces. Place on a tray and sprinkle with the sea. Ensure the ribs are completely covered. Leave in the fridge for 1 hour.

Remove the ribs from the tray and rinse under cold running water to remove the salt.

Preheat the oven to 120°C/100°C fan/Gas Mark ½. Lay the ribs in a deep ovenproof tray or tin and pour over cold water to cover. Add the garlic, thyme, bay leaves, star anise and cloves. Cover with foil. Place the tray in the oven and cook for 2–2½ hours or until the rib meat is very tender but not falling from the bone. The low temperature should be monitored to ensure the ribs do not cook too quickly – check 2 or 3 times during cooking and skim off any scum that has risen to the surface.

Meanwhile, put the quince paste, coriander seeds, smoked paprika and 100ml of water in a saucepan and melt slowly over a low heat to make a thick glaze. Set aside.

When the ribs are cooked, remove them from the oven and leave to cool down in the cooking liquor. Once cool, drain the ribs well (reserve the cooking liquor for another use, such as in a sauce or soup) and place them on a tray. Pour over most of the quince glaze (reserve some for basting later) and toss through the ribs to coat them.

When you are ready to serve, you can either finish the ribs on the barbecue, over hot coals, or on a hot ridged grill pan. Barbecue or grill the ribs for 3–4 minutes on each side or until they are evenly caramelised and hot. Baste with the remaining quince glaze as you go. Season with sea salt, sprinkle over the toasted flaked almonds and coriander, and serve.

Braised Pork Collar
with Almond Milk, Dates and Saffron

This aromatic slow-cooked braise is reminiscent of a tagine in terms of its consistency, and is yet another wonderful example of how the Moors left their culinary stamp in Spain.

The Arabs would have originally used lamb neck or belly for this dish, or failing that plump wood pigeons, whose slightly bitter-tannic flavour would have been offset by the sweetness of the dates and almond milk.

I use Medjool dates which have a good level of natural sweetness and a chewy, sticky consistency. When cooked, the sweetness turns to a delicious deep caramel, enriching the whole dish.

Often put through a mincer for sausages in the UK, the pork collar is a much-underused part of the pig. The Spaniards have a different take on pork butchery and love utilising even the most obscure pieces of the beast.

When carefully slow-cooked this dish is a real gem, perfect to put on and cook gently and long through a cold afternoon.

Serves 6–8

olive oil
1 x 2kg boneless pork collar
  roasting joint
1 large onion, finely sliced
3 garlic cloves, chopped
30g ground almonds
1 litre chicken stock (home-made
  or ready-made fresh)

12 Medjool dates, pitted
2 pinches of saffron threads
1 litre almond milk
50g flat-leaf parsley, finely chopped
50g flaked almonds, lightly toasted
sea salt and black pepper

Preheat the oven to 160°C/140°C fan/Gas Mark 3.

Set a large flameproof casserole over a medium heat and add a glug of oil. Sear the pork collar in the hot oil to brown on all sides. Remove from the pot. Add the onion and garlic and cook until softened and lightly coloured. Stir in the ground almonds plus a little more oil and cook for 2 minutes.

Return the pork to the pot and pour in the chicken stock. Bring the stock to the boil and reduce by about half, skimming off any impurities that rise to the surface. Now add the dates, saffron threads, almond milk and plenty of seasoning. Bring back to the boil. Cover the casserole and transfer to the oven. Cook for 2 hours or until the pork is very tender and the stock has reduced to a thick yellow sauce. If the sauce is still too thin, place the casserole on the hob and boil rapidly, uncovered, over a high heat to reduce.

Leave the pork to rest in the sauce in the covered casserole for at least 30 minutes before serving. Scatter the chopped parsley and toasted almonds over the pork and serve in the casserole, family style at the table. I like to serve this with steamed rice or cous cous.

Pig's Cheeks
with Garlic and Cumin Potatoes

Spaniards know their pork well and they know what to do with the best cuts.

Pigs' cheeks are the perfect slow-cooker. The cheeks hold their shape during a long, slow braise, and have the most incredible lip-smacking unctuousness, their natural gelatine adding rich body to the cooking liquor.

The addition of orange zest and spice are a throw back to the Moorish days when the precursor to this dish would have been made with lamb and dried fruits, not unlike a North African tagine.

When buying from your butcher, be sure to ask for 'the spots' which are the nuggets of meat found in the jowl.

Serves 4

Cheeks
olive oil
8 large pig's cheek spots, cut from
  the jowl
2 carrots, chopped
1 large onion, chopped
1 celery stick, chopped
4 garlic cloves, crushed
3 bay leaves
500ml dry sherry
2 star anise
pared zest of ½ orange

6 sprigs of thyme
1.5 litres pork or dark chicken stock
  (home-made or ready-made fresh)
sea salt and black pepper

Potatoes
600g Desiree potatoes, peeled and cut
  into bite-size chunks
olive oil
1 teaspoon cumin seeds, lightly
  crushed
3 garlic cloves, finely chopped

Preheat the oven to 140°C/120°C fan/Gas Mark 1.

Heat a heavy flameproof casserole over a medium heat. Add a glug of oil and then the cheeks and brown them on both sides, creating a deep, rich crust. Remove the cheeks to a bowl. Add the vegetables, garlic and bay leaves to the pot and cook for a few minutes to caramelise.

Return the cheeks to the pot along with the sherry, star anise, orange zest and thyme. Turn up the heat and boil the sherry to reduce by two thirds. Pour in the stock and bring back to the boil, skimming off any scum that forms on the surface. Cover the casserole and transfer to the oven. Cook for about 2 hours or until the cheeks are very tender (if you can cut them with a spoon, they are ready) and the cooking liquor has reduced to a rich, thick sauce consistency. If the sauce is still too thin you can put the casserole back on the hob and boil to reduce the liquor to the desired consistency.

An hour before the cheeks are ready, cook the potatoes in boiling salted water until just tender. Drain well and spread out on an oven tray to cool.

...continued on page 164

Remove the casserole from the oven and leave to rest, covered, while you roast the potatoes. (The resting is important to let everything relax and develop the flavours – there will still be enough heat left to serve later.)

Turn up the oven to 200°C/180°C fan/Gas Mark 6. Drizzle olive oil over the potatoes, season and sprinkle over the cumin. Place in the oven and roast for 25 minutes or until the potatoes are browning and turning crisp. Sprinkle over the garlic and toss through the potatoes. Continue roasting for 10 minutes or until crisp. Season again.

I like to serve this in the classic Andalucían way – in individual bowls with the potatoes in first, topped with the cheeks and sauce. The potatoes will become soft from the sauce, making them all the more delicious.

Braised Oxtail
with Chorizo, Red Wine and Soffrito

This dish is perhaps the heartiest of meat stews I know – braised oxtails reinforced with red wine, sherry, spices and fiery chorizo. It's a dish to be cooked and savoured on the coldest of winter days, able to warm both the kitchen and the soul.

This is a dish that must be planned and made hours in advance. Not only does the oxtail take a good while to tenderise but the braise must rest well in order to allow the flavours to develop fully. Traditional recipes call for a 48-hour process to achieve the best results though I think a good day to make will give you something quite special.

The Moors love of slow-cooked, spiced stews would certainly have influenced the origins of this dish. The addition of alcohol and chorizo would have come at a later date with the Andalucíans using what they had to hand to make the dish tasty and help it go further in leaner times. The chorizo would have been used as a bulker but what a genius idea – not only does it add bulk but it also adds flavour while the delicious spicy pork fat enriches the braising liquor.

Serves 4

1.5kg oxtail, cut into sections and fat trimmed (your butcher will prepare this for you)
1 tablespoon plain flour
olive oil
1 onion, chopped
1 large carrot, chopped
1 large celery stick, chopped
4 garlic cloves, roughly chopped
1 cinnamon stick
1 teaspoon hot smoked paprika

1 teaspoon ground cumin
2 bay leaves
200g spicy cooking chorizo, peeled and roughly chopped
1 tablespoon tomato purée
½ bottle of red wine
50ml dry sherry (optional)
500ml beef stock (home-made or ready-made fresh)
300g ripe tomatoes, chopped
sea salt and black pepper

Heat a large flameproof casserole over a medium heat. Dust the oxtail pieces with flour and shake off the excess. Add a glug of oil to the pot followed by the oxtail. Brown the pieces on all sides, then remove them from the pot.

Preheat the oven to 140°C/120°C fan/Gas Mark 1.

Add the chopped onion, carrot, celery and garlic to the casserole and cook this soffrito for a few minutes to brown and soften. Next add the cinnamon stick, paprika, cumin and bay leaves and cook for a couple of minutes before adding the chorizo. Cook until it releases its fatty juices. Stir in the tomato purée and cook for a couple of minutes before pouring in the wine and sherry. Bring to the boil, scraping the bottom of the pot to release any sediments into the sauce. Boil the liquid to reduce by two thirds.

...continued on page 166

Return the oxtail pieces to the pot and pour in the stock and chopped tomatoes. Bring back to the boil, skimming off any scum that rises to the surface. Cover the casserole and transfer to the oven. Cook for 3–3½ hours or until the meat is falling from the bone and the liquid has a deep, rich sauce consistency. (If the sauce is a little too thin, boil it down on the hob until it thickens.)

Leave the stew to stand (covered) for at least 1½ hours before serving – this will allow the flavours to develop. Then taste and add salt and pepper as necessary.

Warm through and serve at the table for everyone to help themselves. My crisp Olive Oil-roasted Potatoes (see page 110) is a classic accompaniment to this dish. In Andalucía the stew is served atop chips in most restaurants. It's delicious but I prefer my chips on the side so they stay crispy!

Beef Cheeks
with Quince, Bay Leaves, Cinnamon and Arbequina Olive Mash

I think of slow-cooked beef cheeks as the ultimate comfort food. Cooked long and slow they turn into the most wonderful, unctuous and flavourful chunks of protein.

This dish was inspired by a gastronomic trip to the town of Arcos de la Frontera in Andalucía. It's a beautiful 11th century Moorish stronghold where the North African influences are felt everywhere. I love how the use of spices and fruits in the cooking adds a depth and exotic sweetness. The rich, indulgent mash works perfectly with the beef.

Serves 4

4 small beef cheeks, sinew removed
500ml red wine
3 bay leaves
2 garlic cloves, crushed
4 shallots, cut in half
olive oil
700ml beef stock (home-made
   or ready-made fresh)
1 cinnamon stick
3 cloves
50ml honey

pared zest of ½ orange
1 quince, peeled, quartered and cored
sea salt and black pepper

Mash
2 large Desiree potatoes, peeled and
   evenly diced
75ml double cream
20g unsalted butter, diced
100ml Arbequina olive oil (or another
   fresh grassy olive oil)

Put the beef cheeks in a dish and cover with the wine. Add the bay leaves, garlic and shallots. Leave to marinate for 6 hours or overnight.

Preheat the oven to 130°C/110°C fan/Gas Mark ¾. Remove the beef cheeks from the marinade and pour the liquid into a flameproof casserole. Set the casserole over a high heat, bring the liquid to the boil and leave to reduce by three-quarters.

Heat a sauté pan over a high heat, add a glug of olive oil and brown the cheeks for 4 minutes on each side or until caramelised. Transfer the cheeks to the reducing marinade. When it has reduced by three-quarters, pour in the stock and add the cinnamon stick, cloves and honey. Bring back to the boil, then cover the casserole and transfer to the oven. Cook for about 2 hours.

Add the orange zest and quince pieces. Cook, covered, for a further 1 hour or until the cheeks and quince are soft and tender. Every so often skim any fat from the surface of the cooking liquid.

Meanwhile, make the mash. Cook the potatoes gently in simmering salted water until tender. Drain and pass through a sieve or vegetable mill into a clean pan. Heat the cream and pour into the potato, then add the diced butter and olive oil. Mix together well. Season to taste and keep warm.

Taste the beef cheek sauce and adjust the seasoning, if necessary. Serve each person a beef cheek and piece of quince with the sauce and a spoonful of mash.

Sherry-glazed Overnight Short Rib of Beef
with Blackened Onions, Yoghurt and Za'atar

Short ribs always need to be cooked long and slow. Cooking them overnight in stock and sweet PX sherry not only tenderises the meat but also produces a sweet, sticky glaze full of meaty goodness from the bones. The blackened bitter onions are a great contrast to the cooling, fresh yoghurt. Za'atar is the name for both a type of thyme grown in the Middle East and also the name for a spice mix used in Middle Eastern cuisine, containing hyssop, sumac, sesame seeds and salt. It is widely available and great to add a spicy crunch to a dish.

Serves 4

olive oil
6 thick, meaty beef short ribs
1 bulb of garlic, cut in half
   horizontally
1 tablespoon tomato purée
½ bottle of red wine
500ml Pedro Ximinez (PX) sherry

1.5 litres fresh beef stock
a bunch of large, spring onions,
a small handful of flat-leaf parsley,
   finely chopped
200ml thick plain yoghurt
2 teaspoons za'atar
sea salt and black pepper

Preheat the oven to 130°C/110°C fan/Gas Mark ¾.

Heat a large flameproof oven tray or lidded casserole over a medium heat (this vessel needs to be big enough to house all the ribs). Add a glug of oil and, when hot, brown the short ribs all over – do this in batches, if necessary, and take your time to ensure the ribs are really nicely caramelised. This is key for a successful dish. When the ribs are all browned and removed from the tray or pot, nestle the garlic in the bottom and add the tomato purée. Cook for 2 minutes, stirring. Return all the ribs to the tray. Pour in the wine and sherry and bring to the boil. Reduce by a half, scraping the bottom of the tray as you go to deglaze.

Add the stock and bring back to the boil, skimming off any impurities that rise to the surface. Cover the tray with foil, or put the lid on the casserole, and transfer to the oven. Cook for 6–7 hours (I put this in before I go to bed and take it out first thing in the morning). The rib meat will be incredibly tender and the liquid quite thick, sticky and rich.

Remove the tray or pot from the oven and turn the oven up to 220°C/200°C fan/Gas Mark 7. Leave the ribs to cool down in the liquid – this will rest the meat and also let the flavours in the sauce develop. Pick out the 2 pieces of garlic bulb and press through a sieve. Stir the resulting garlic purée into the sauce.

While the ribs are cooling, trim the spring onions and toss with some oil and seasoning. Place in a roasting tray and roast for about 20 minutes or until tender and charred.

When ready to serve, slowly heat up the ribs in the tray or casserole. If the sauce seems too thick, add a splash of stock or water. When hot, check the seasoning and stir in the parsley.

Spoon the yoghurt on to a plate and top with the onions. Serve the ribs family style at the table sprinkled with the za'atar.

Pastilla

The pastilla ('small pie') evolved after the Moorish occupation ended and their subsequent expulsion back to North Africa. These were turbulent times that witnessed many changes and movement of peoples, with some Andalucíans deciding to flee across the seas to Morocco for a new life. This exodus created a whole subculture of immigrant Andalucíans influencing the long-established cuisine of North Africa.

So a dish from North Africa influenced by the immigrant Andalucíans – a flip side of the subject of this book yet perfectly illustrating the universal culinary truth of how cultures never stand still and always take from the communities within for a greater culinary good.

The pastilla is usually filled with squab pigeon or chicken, flavoured with dried fruits, nuts and spices, and finished with a final dusting of icing sugar.

Serves 4

olive oil
2 oven-ready squab pigeons, about
    500g in total, each cut in half (or
    500g chicken pieces – a mix of
    breast and thigh/leg on the bone)
1 onion, finely chopped
2 cinnamon sticks
4 garlic cloves, finely sliced
2 dried red chillies
1 chipotle chilli
40g stoned Medjool dates, chopped

1 teaspoon pink peppercorns
75ml brandy
200ml white wine
300ml dark chicken stock
2 plum tomatoes, each quartered
10g dark chocolate (with 70%
    cocoa solids)
4 tablespoons ghee or clarified butter
140g filo pastry (10–12 sheets)
icing sugar, to dust
sea salt and black pepper

For the best results (and flavour), make the filling for the pie the day before you want to assemble and cook it.

Preheat the oven to 150°C/130°C fan/Gas Mark 2.

Heat a large flameproof casserole over a medium heat and add glug of olive oil. When hot, brown the pigeon (or chicken) pieces all over – do this in batches, if necessary, so you don't overcrowd the pot. Set the browned pigeon pieces aside to drain.

Add more oil to the pot, then add the onion, cinnamon, garlic and all the chillies. Cook for 2 minutes, stirring. Return the pigeon to the pot along with the dates, peppercorns, brandy and wine. Boil to reduce the liquid to a syrup, then add the stock and tomatoes. Bring back to the boil. Skim off impurities, then turn the heat down to a simmer. Add the chocolate.

Put the lid on the casserole and transfer to the oven. Cook for 2 hours or until the meat is very tender and the cooking liquor is rich with a sauce-like consistency. Remove from the oven and cool.

…continued on page 174

When cool, pick out the pieces of pigeon and take the meat off the bone; discard the skin. Stir the meat back into the sauce, which should be thick. If it seems too liquid, set the pot over a high heat and boil to reduce to a saucy glaze, then leave to cool again. Keep the filling in the fridge until the next day.

You need a 15cm round pie dish/tin or similar to mould this pastilla. Remove the filling from the fridge to come to room temperature.

Preheat the oven to 170°C/150°C fan/Gas Mark 3½.

Melt the ghee or butter in a small saucepan and have ready a pastry brush for this. Layer 3 sheets of filo pastry on your worktop, brushing each on the top side with ghee and placing them at an angle to create a star. Take another sheet of filo and cut it into 4 squares. Brush each of these on one side with ghee, then layer them on top of each other. Place in the centre of the layered filo star to create a base. Transfer this to the pie dish, pressing in the pastry at the sides and leaving a good overhang all around the rim.

Spoon the filling into the pastry case. Fold the overhanging filo over the top and brush it with ghee. Brush 2 sheets of filo on one side with ghee, then stick them together. Cut to fit the top of the pie to seal completely and stick in place, using more ghee if necessary. Brush the top with the last of the ghee.

Place the pie in the oven and bake for 25 minutes or until the top starts to become brown and crisp. Now carefully, holding the dish with an oven cloth, flip the pie out on to a baking sheet. Place back in the oven to bake for a further 10–15 minutes or until the pastry is completely golden brown and crisp and the filling is piping hot.

Dust with icing sugar and serve immediately to cut at the table.

Pot-roasted Quails
with Lemon Leaves, White Beans and Pomegranate

Not really a slow-cooked recipe but it feels like the right chapter to include this fresh southern Italian inspired dish. Pot-roasting is usually associated with larger and more dense meats where the simultaneous process of steaming and roasting helps keep things nice and moist while the flesh tenderises over time. I've found the process also works very well for these little quails – they brown nicely, stay moist and also pick up the flavours of the fresh, aromatic lemon leaves.

We don't really associate lemon leaves with cooking nowadays but long ago they were used to protect delicate meat and fish when cooking over a fierce open fire naturally imparting a citrusy perfume. It's still a popular practice in Sicily to wrap veal and delicate fish in lemon leaves before grilling on a barbecue. Fresh leafy lemons are available in the winter months but you can buy dried ones that just need to be rehydrated.

Serves 4

olive oil
4 plump oven-ready quails
4 sprigs of lemon thyme or thyme
12–16 large lemon leaves (fresh
  or dried)
175ml white wine
2 garlic cloves, crushed

1 x 400g can cannellini or other white
  beans, drained and rinsed
grated zest and juice of ½ lemon
seeds from ½ pomegranate
50ml pomegranate molasses
sea salt and black pepper

Preheat the oven to 180°C/160°C fan/Gas Mark 4.

Place a flameproof casserole large enough to hold the quails over a medium heat and add a good glug of olive oil. Season the quails and push a sprig of thyme into the cavity of each bird. Brown them evenly on all sides in the hot oil. Remove from the heat.

Lift the quails out of the pot and wrap each one in 3 or 4 lemon leaves, securing with wooden cocktail sticks. Place the quails back in the pot, set it over the heat again and add the wine and garlic. Bring to the boil. Cover the casserole tightly and transfer to the oven. Cook for 25 minutes.

Take the casserole out of the oven and leave covered for 10 minutes before removing the quails to a warm spot to rest. Set the pot back on a medium heat on the hob and bring the cooking juices to the boil. Reduce by half. Add the beans, lemon zest and juice, pomegranate seeds and pomegranate molasses and season well. Cook for a couple of minutes to heat everything through. Pour any quail resting juices into the pot and stir in.

Remove the cocktail sticks from the quails but keep the lemon leaves in place. Serve the braised beans on the side.

SWEET & SOUR

I am slightly obsessed with the gastronomic marriage of sweet and sour, a combination beloved by both the Arabs and the Jews of Moorish Spain. When perfectly balanced I believe it to be the ultimate taste sensation.

At its most basic, the addition of a pinch of sugar and a squeeze of lemon or drop of vinegar can add so much more to a dish than the sum of the simple parts. The combination, when perfectly in tune, can harmonise and mollify a dish, adding complexity and backbone.

The Moorish influence sees many dishes brought together with the combination of sweet and sour. The Moors had a fondness for the sourness of citrus fruits and vinegars, which both acted as natural coolants in the blazing heat and also as preservers and picklers which, before refrigeration, was essential for preserving. Pickling is without question one of the most significant gastronomic influences that the Moors brought to the Iberian peninsula.

Before the arrival of sugar cane the natural sweetener was honey which the Arabs used in abundance. Honey is still one of the most used ingredients in Moorish cooking, going hand in hand with molasses and refined sugars.

For me, the sweet and sour dishes included in this book evoke the very essence of Moorish cuisine. A magical combination borne out of necessity that became forever intertwined with the cultures of the region.

I love the discipline of creating natural sweet and sour combinations from given ingredients, often utilising natural sugars to create wonderful dishes. Carrots for example are naturally sweet, especially when cooked, so the addition of a little vinegar during or after cooking can work a special magic.

I've always had a love for vinegars and pickles which I suspect is a passion passed down through generations of family palates going way back to my Eastern European roots. My restaurant kitchens always stock far more types of vinegar than is necessary and I will often find myself adding small drops here and there to season, just as you might with a little salt and pepper. There are so many wonderful varieties of vinegars available now, from the basic red and white wine vinegars to the grape-specific cabernet sauvignon, merlot and Riesling or sherry, balsamic, apple, moscatel and beyond.

Other natural sweet and sour wizardry comes in the form of fruit molasses such as pomegranate, the juice of fresh pomegranates reduced to a sticky, sweet syrup to create a fresh acidity – instant sweet and sour. If you can find saba (grape must) use it to add to drinks and marinades – clean and fresh tasting with a lovely sweet and sour balance.

Gordal Olives
Stuffed with Orange, Goat's Curd and Cumin Salt

Gordal or 'fat' olives are grown and processed in the Seville region of southern Spain. Large with a crisp texture and a naturally sweet flavour, they are ideal for stuffing.

This is in many ways the perfect tapas dish, simple to prepare, delicious to eat and a perfect gastronomic gateway to many more delicious tapas dishes.

I like to fill these olives with a creamy goat's curd (though any good soft cheese would work well) and some sweet-sour orange and cumin spice – all very much a throw back to the Moorish occupation.

When imported the tinned variety olives often come packed in brine stuffed with spicy Guindilla peppers, giving a pleasant and unexpected little kick.

Makes 20

20 pitted Gordal olives, drained
1 teaspoon cumin seeds
2 teaspoons sea salt
30g goat's curd

1 small orange, peel and pith removed, then segmented
extra virgin olive oil

Cut each olive lengthways through the middle to open up the cavity, leaving the underside intact and joined together. Turn the olive over and trim a small slice from the base – this will create a small flat area so the olive won't roll over when serving.

Lightly crush the cumin seeds in a bowl, or with a pestle and mortar, and mix into the salt.

Whisk the goat's curd to ensure it is smooth, then spoon into a small piping bag and pipe carefully into the olive cavities, swirling the curd from the top. Alternatively, you can fill the cavities using a teaspoon, although it won't give the same finish.

Cut each orange segment into 3 or 4 pieces, dependent on size, and nestle a piece in the goat's curd in each olive. Sprinkle the olives liberally with the cumin salt and drizzle over some extra virgin olive oil, then serve.

Caramelised Chicory
with Saba and Orange

Chicory leaves are often found in bitter salads or simply braised with some butter and stock. This treatment is a revelation, where the juicy, bitter leaves are tempered and sweetened via the cooking process, allowing the natural sugars to turn to a sticky caramel.

I first tried barbecued chicory in Sicily – the heads were cooked over olive wood until sticky and slightly charred, then drizzled with almond milk and orange. My version keeps the orange (it has a natural affinity with chicory) and adds a drizzle of grape must (saba) which, if you can't find, simply substitute with pomegranate molasses or an aged balsamic.

Serves 4

4 heads red chicory
3 heads yellow chicory
olive oil
2 tablespoons saba (see above)

2 small blood oranges (or 1 large sweet orange), skin and pith removed, then segmented
sea salt and black pepper

Heat a ridged grill pan over a medium heat, or prepare and light a charcoal fire in a barbecue.

Cut each head of chicory into quarters lengthways. The yellow chicory will likely be bigger with a thicker stalk, so trim any excess stalk.

Rub the chicory with olive oil and season well. Place on the hot pan or barbecue and cook for 3 minutes on each side to soften and char. Don't be afraid to blacken the leaves here – chicory really benefits from the flavour this gives.

When the chicory has softened, you should be able to splay out the leaves like a fan. Cook like this for a further 2 minutes on each side. Transfer to a serving dish. Drizzle with the saba and scatter over the orange segments before serving.

Pickled Carrots
with Coriander

I may well be asking for trouble when I say that the Andalucíans don't do vegetables particularly well. It's not that there's a shortage of beautiful fresh produce growing locally – there's lots and lots of lovely stuff – it's just that protein takes centre stage.

However, one vegetable dish you will find in many of the tapas bars is a version of these pickled carrots; a leftover gem from the Moorish occupation where vegetables were soused to prolong life. The Moors adored the heady, satisfying hit of sweet-sour flavours.

Though this is a simple preparation you must be vigilant and be sure to use the very best quality ingredients available in order to permit the dish to sing.

I like to serve the carrots chilled straight from the fridge.

Serves 6–8
as a snack or as part of
a tapas/mezze spread

1½ tablespoons sea salt
450g heritage carrots, peeled and cut
    into 1cm slices
250ml good-quality cider vinegar
    (preferably organic)

50g caster sugar
1 garlic clove, crushed
1½ tablespoons coriander seeds,
    lightly crushed
a handful of coriander leaves, to serve

Add the salt to a saucepan of water and bring to the boil. Add the carrots. Blanch for 2 minutes, then drain and refresh the carrots under cold running water until fully cold. Pat dry with a tea towel.

Put the remaining ingredients (except the coriander leaves) in the saucepan and add 310ml of water. Bring to the boil, then simmer for 2 minutes to infuse the flavours. Remove from the heat. Add the blanched carrots and leave to cool completely at room temperature.

Transfer the carrots and cooking liquor to sterilised jars. Cover and leave to pickle in the fridge for at least 24 hours. They will keep well in the fridge for up to 6 weeks.

Serve chilled, in pots with some of the liquor, sprinkled with fresh coriander leaves. Accompany with some bread and soft sheep's or goat's cheese. Delicious.

Pumpkin Caponata
with Fresh Marjoram

A trip to Sicily is incomplete without sampling the classic caponata that abounds all across the island. I have spent many happy hours trying the different local versions. Simple to make with the giveaway signs of Arabic influence in the use of fruits and nuts and addition of vinegar as a flavouring and a preservative.

My recipe is unusual in that it contains roasted pumpkin – the vegetable's extra sweetness and texture works really well. The inspired addition of coco powder was prompted by a version that I tried at a restaurant called Tischi-Toshi in Taormina, it was without doubt the best caponata that I'd ever eaten until I came up with this version in my kitchen at home in London a few weeks later!

Serves 6–8

extra virgin olive oil
250g peeled heavy-fleshed pumpkin
   (such as ironbark), cut into 2cm dice
2 onions, finely sliced
1 large courgette, cut into 2cm dice
1 celery stick, cut into 2cm dice
200g fresh plum tomatoes,
   roughly chopped
200g canned chopped tomatoes

100ml red wine vinegar
30g small capers
20g cocoa powder
1 tablespoon caster sugar
50g raisins
40g pine nuts, toasted
a good handful of picked
   marjoram leaves
sea salt and black pepper

Preheat the oven to 220°C/200°C fan/Gas Mark 7.

Pour 1cm of extra virgin olive oil into a deep-sided baking tray and place this in the hot oven. When the oil is hot, carefully add the pumpkin dice with some seasoning. Return to the oven and roast for 25 minutes or until the pumpkin is golden brown and tender. Remove the pumpkin from the oil using a slotted spoon and drain on kitchen paper.

Heat a large flameproof casserole over a medium heat. Add a good glug of extra virgin olive oil and then the onions. Cook slowly until they are tender and caramelised before adding the courgette and celery. Cook for a further 5 minutes or until the courgette is softened. Add the fresh and canned tomatoes. Simmer for 10 minutes or until the tomatoes have broken down and the sauce is thick and rich.

Add the roasted pumpkin along with the vinegar, capers, cocoa, sugar and plenty of seasoning. Cook for 5 minutes, stirring to mix everything. Remove from the heat and stir in the raisins and pine nuts. Cover with a lid or foil, then leave to rest for at least 1 hour.

Stir in the marjoram leaves. Serve at room temperature with some warm crostini sprinkled with olive oil and sea salt.

Top left: Pumpkin Caponata with Fresh Marjoram (see page 185)
Bottom left: Pickled Carrots with Coriander (see page 184)
Right: Mullet in Saffron Escabeche (see page 188)

Mullet in Saffron Escabeche

Variations of escabeche appear in many countries throughout the world but is perhaps best known throughout the towns and villages of southern Spain.

Escabeche or scabetche is a variation on the pickling and preserving method introduced by the Arabs as a way of keeping foods longer in the heat. Escabeche differs from most pickling in that the pickling liquor and the food being pickled come together to make a whole dish. The pickle becomes the sauce and the chosen food is then broken down into it, rather like a coarse, piquant pâté.

Escabeche is one of the most delicious things to have on hand when kept in a jar in the fridge. I can be found making escabeche throughout the year, and I like to use seasonal produce such as pheasant or partridge as well as the stronger, more robust fish such as mackerel that can withstand the attack of strong flavours from the pickle. I've included carrots here to add an extra sweetness to help counter the astringency of the vinegar.

Serves 4

1 large carrot, peeled and finely sliced
2 banana shallots, finely sliced
2 bay leaves
1 star anise
1 teaspoon coriander seeds
150ml extra virgin olive oil (such as Arbequina)
250ml moscatel vinegar or white balsamic

6 saffron threads
olive oil
4 large fillets red or grey mullet, pin-boned and each cut in half crossways
a squeeze of lemon
sea salt and black pepper

Put the carrot, shallots, bay leaves, star anise and coriander seeds in a saucepan and pour in the extra virgin olive oil and vinegar. Bring slowly to the boil. Add the saffron and season to taste. Turn down the heat and simmer for 2 minutes. Remove this marinade from the heat and set aside.

Heat a non-stick pan over a high heat and add a glug of olive oil. Season the mullet pieces and place in the pan skin side down. Cook until the skin is browned and crisp. Remove the fish from the pan and place in a plastic or glass container. Pour over the marinade and add a squeeze of lemon juice. The fillets should be completely submerged.

Cover the container and leave to pickle in the fridge for at least 2 hours and up to 3 weeks. Before serving, remove the escabeche from the fridge to come up to room temperature.

I've enjoyed this as part of a mezze-style feast. My Roasted Beetroots and Carrots (see page 142) works particularly well with the escabeche.

Albondigas
in an Almond and Sherry Vinegar Sauce

Albondigas is the pleasingly evocative Spanish word for meatballs. There are endless recipes claiming to be the definitive Holy Grail version, but it's subjective.

Lamb albondigas would be more in keeping with the Moorish culture but I love a beef meatball and in this recipe I've added some fatty chorizo to the mix for extra lubrication and zing.

The almond-bread sauce is typical of the Andalucían-Moorish thickening combinations and is often served cold in the Andalucían ajo blanco soup (see page 281). I love these rich sauces but the intense sweetness demands a good hit of acidity for balance – here some excellent aged sherry vinegar does just that.

Serves 4

Albondigas
550g best-quality beef mince
125g spicy chorizo
15g dried breadcrumbs
6 tablespoons milk
2 garlic cloves, finely chopped
½ teaspoon hot smoked paprika
a small bunch of flat-leaf parsley,
    chopped, plus extra to garnish
1 small egg, beaten
olive oil
2 bay leaves
sea salt and black pepper

Almond and sherry vinegar sauce
25ml extra virgin olive oil
2 slices day-old white bread, crusts
    removed, cut into bite-size pieces
40g ground almonds
1 garlic clove, finely chopped
60ml white wine
60ml best-quality sweet sherry vinegar
300ml chicken stock (home-made
    is best)

Put the beef mince in a bowl and season well with salt and pepper. Combine the chorizo, breadcrumbs, milk, garlic, smoked paprika and parsley in a food processor and blitz to form a rough paste. Add the chorizo mixture to the beef along with the egg. Mix together very well to ensure everything is thoroughly amalgamated.

Form the mince mix into 28 balls and chill in the fridge for at least 1 hour.

Heat a large non-stick sauté pan over a medium heat and add a glug of olive oil. Fry the meatballs with the bay leaves in 2 batches until they are nicely browned all over. Transfer to a dish (discard the bay leaves).

Make the sauce in the same pan. Add the extra virgin olive oil to the pan, then add the bread, almonds and garlic and cook, stirring, for a few minutes over a medium heat until lightly coloured. Add the wine and vinegar and bring to the boil, then reduce by three-quarters. Pour in the stock and bring back to the boil, then turn down to a simmer. Return the meatballs to the pan and cook in the simmering sauce for 10 minutes or until they are just cooked through and the sauce has thickened.

Serve sprinkled with more chopped parsley.

Anchovies
with Orange, Thyme, Mint and Pepper

Anchovies are like Marmite – you will either love them or hate them. However, the haters probably haven't tried the magnificent plump white boquerones that are landed all around southern Spain. Their texture is firm and their flesh meaty. They are often marinated in a light oil and vinegar mix, which adds just a note of acidity helping the fish to hold their shape and retain their consistency.

The preserving process for anchovies is little changed over the centuries – salt, vinegar, oil and that's pretty much it. But what was once a simple and necessary process of preservation has become a celebration of taste and texture.

The classic light neutral-pickle used encourages the addition of further flavours. Here I've used the never failing combination of thyme and mint, heavily seasoned with lots of freshly ground black pepper – less pepper is definitely not more in this recipe.

Good fresh anchovies are hard to find in the UK, unlike in Spain where they are found in abundance at local markets. Source the best white boquerones you can find – I suggest Brindisa in the UK, who have a great online shop and stock excellent Nardin and Ortiz anchovies. Ensure you buy the pickled variety for this recipe as opposed to the salted.

I can and do eat these beauties by the plateful accompanied by a glass or two of chilled bone-dry fino.

Serves 4
as part of a mezze

1 x 150g tray lightly pickled
    white boquerones
1 teaspoon picked thyme leaves
½ teaspoon freshly ground
    black pepper
75ml extra virgin olive oil

½ teaspoon caster sugar
50ml sweet white vinegar (white
    balsamic or moscatel)
1 small sweet orange
a handful of mint leaves, roughly torn
sea salt

Drain the anchovies well from their brine and carefully dab them dry with kitchen paper. Place the anchovies in a dish and sprinkle over the thyme, pepper and salt to taste.

Whisk together the oil, sugar and vinegar. Peel and segment the orange, reserving any juices. Cut each segment into 2 or 3 pieces and scatter over the fish. Whisk the orange juice into the vinaigrette and pour over the anchovies. Leave in the fridge to marinate for at least an hour.

About 20 minutes before eating, remove the anchovies from the fridge to bring to room temperature. Scatter over the mint and serve. Some warm crostini is good to serve them on, if you wish.

Sardines al Saor

Sardines al soar is a renowned classic Venetian cicchetti (small dish) reportedly first created in the 12th century. The preparation is designed to prolong the life of the fish and was taken to sea by the spice merchants and sailors to feed and nourish themselves on long journeys away from port.

Though the dish is not strictly Moorish, the influences are apparent – preserving, sweetness from fruits and the addition of nuts and spices.

I suspect that the Venetians would go to battle over any attempt to claim this dish for the Moors but it is such a lovely plate of food that I can't bring myself to exclude it – so I will just have to be prepared to take up culinary cudgels to protect its place and honour within these covers.

Traditionally it would have been made to preserve fish just past its best but I would strongly encourage using the freshest sardines you can find!

Serves 4

olive oil
50g unsalted butter
2 onions, finely sliced
2 bay leaves
3 cloves
1 cinnamon stick
½ teaspoon ground ginger

1 tablespoon demerara sugar
1 tablespoon raisins
2 tablespoons white wine vinegar
8 large sardines, butterflied
1 tablespoon chopped flat-leaf parsley
sea salt and black pepper

Preheat the grill to high.

Set a medium saucepan over a medium heat and add a glug of olive oil and the butter. When the butter foams, add the onions, bay leaves, spices and sugar. Cook over a moderate heat for 30 minutes or until the onions are very soft and lightly coloured. Stir in the raisins and vinegar. Reduce until syrupy. Season well, then remove from the heat and set aside to cool.

Arrange the sardines flesh side down on a non-stick baking tray. Drizzle over a little olive oil and season. Place under the grill and cook for 2 minutes, leaving the flesh still pink.

Spread half the onion mix on a large plate or tray and top with a layer of the sardines. Cover them with the rest of the onion mix. Cover and leave to marinate in the fridge for at least 4 hours.

Before serving, bring the sardines up to room temperature. Divide among serving plates and sprinkle with parsley. Delicious served with hot flatbreads.

Chicken Livers
with Sticky Figs and PX Sherry

I find that fried chicken livers are in need of a sweet-sour combo to counterbalance their naturally bitter, tannic flavour. The slow-baked figs I've used here, when combined with the sherry vinegar and syrupy PX sherry, do the job perfectly. PX is the sweetest of the sherry varieties – thick, dark and sticky, full of wonderful mulled flavours and a world away from the bone-dry, lighter finos drunk in the tapas bars of Spain.

I marinate the livers in spiced buttermilk to draw out any impurities and then toss them through seasoned flour before frying – this trick gives the most delicious spice-scented crust while keeping the livers moist and pink within.

Serves 4
as a starter

½ teaspoon fennel seeds
½ teaspoon cumin seeds
½ teaspoon coriander seeds
¼ teaspoon ground cinnamon
200ml buttermilk
400g chicken livers, trimmed of any
    sinew and fat
75g plain flour
olive oil
sea salt and black pepper

Figs
3 large, ripe black figs, cut in
    half lengthways
50ml sherry vinegar
1 tablespoon demerara sugar
100ml Pedro Ximinez sherry
grated zest of ½ orange

Place the spices in a small, dry sauté pan and heat for 3 minutes or until they become fragrant and start to release their oils. Immediately transfer to a spice grinder or mortar and grind to a powder. Add the spice powder to the buttermilk in a bowl, season and stir. Add the livers. Leave to marinate for an hour.

Toss the figs with the sherry vinegar, sugar, PX sherry and orange zest on a small baking tray. Set aside to marinate for 30 minutes. Meanwhile, preheat the oven to 160°C/140°C fan/Gas Mark 3.

Place the tray of figs in the oven and cook for 25 minutes or until they have softened and the marinade has turned syrupy. Leave to cool.

Divide the flour into 2 bowls and season. A few at a time, lift the livers out of the buttermilk and dab off any excess with kitchen paper, then dredge the livers in the first bowl of flour. Dip them back into the buttermilk and then into the second bowl of flour, making sure they are completely coated (this double-dip process is messy but well worth it for super crisp and delicious livers).

Heat a large sauté pan over a high heat and add a good amount of oil – you are essentially shallow frying so about 1cm of olive oil. When the oil is hot, fry the livers, in 2 batches, for 2–3 minutes on each side or until crisp and golden brown but still pink inside. Remove with a slotted spoon to kitchen paper to drain. Sprinkle with sea salt and serve hot with the figs and the fig-PX syrup.

Roasted Duck
with Fennel and Sweet and Sour Pickled Green Plums

Green plums are a variety of young, underripe plum – quite sour with a firm, crunchy texture. They need to be cooked or pickled before eating. Green plums are used in Middle Eastern cooking to counterbalance fatty meat stews and add a sweet-sour flavouring in dishes and to transform mouth-puckering sour pickles into delicious condiments.

In my recipe they are sweet pickled with the addition of spices and aromats that work well with the rich, fattiness of the duck. This recipe will make more than you need but their versatility means you could use them as an accompaniment to cold meats and cheeses, chopped into salads or vegetables or used as a condiment for fattier fish like mackerel.

Serves 4–6

1 crown of duck (Barbary or
    Gressingham), about 1.1kg
1 teaspoon ground cinnamon
1 teaspoon ground cumin
1 teaspoon ground coriander
2 bulbs of fennel, cut into
    quarters lengthways
olive oil
sea salt and black pepper

Sweet and sour green plums
250g caster sugar
500ml distilled vinegar
100ml runny honey
4 bay leaves
2 teaspoons green peppercorns
4 dried red chillies
10 cardamom seeds (removed
    from pods)
1kg young, sour green plums

You'll need to make the sweet and sour green plums at least a day in advance. Put the sugar, vinegar, honey and bay leaves in a saucepan and heat until the sugar has dissolved. Add the peppercorns, chillies and cardamom. Simmer for 2 minutes. Remove from the heat.

Pack the plums into 1 or 2 jars, depending on size, and pour over the hot pickling liquid. Ensure the spices and chillies are evenly split between the 2 jars. Put on the lids and seal. Turn the jars upside down and leave for 10 minutes, then turn back upright – this ensures a good seal. Leave to cool. The plums will be ready to eat in 24 hours and will continue to improve over the next 10 days. They can be stored in a cool spot for up to 6 months.

When you want to roast the duck crown, preheat the oven to 210°C/190°C fan/Gas Mark 6½. Lightly score the skin on the breast of the duck, making sure not to cut too deep into the flesh (this will aid the fat rendering during roasting). Season the crown, then rub over the spices. Place the fennel in a baking tray and sit the duck crown on top. Roast for about 55 minutes or until the skin of the duck is brown and crisp, the meat is nice and pink and the fennel is cooked through.

While the duck is roasting, take out as many plums (say, 10–12) as you want to serve. Cut them in half and remove the stones.

Remove the tray from the oven. Pour off the rendered fat and reserve for another later use. Leave the duck to rest for 20 minutes before carving. Serve thick slices of duck with the fennel and the pickled plums.

Ibérico Pork
with Quince, Cumin, Sweet Vinegar and Marjoram

Ibérico or black foot are the king of pigs and are thought to be the oldest known breed. Their diet consists predominantly of acorns, which flavours the meat making it sweet, nutty and succulent. Due to its impeccable heritage, breeding and semi-red/wild meat it's perfectly safe (and all the more delicious) to be eaten rare – I've made Ibérico tartare with great success.

It's a unique product and pleasingly is becoming far more widely available now. If you can't find Ibérico then a decent piece of old spot or lop will suffice nicely.

Serves 4
as part of a
mezze platter

1 x 400g Ibérico pork loin (or good
   heritage-breed pork loin), trimmed
olive oil
1 tablespoon cumin seeds
2 teaspoons sweet smoked paprika
150ml blossom honey
1 quince, peeled and cut into 2cm dice

100ml moscatel vinegar
40g membrillo (quince paste)
200ml dark chicken stock
a small handful of marjoram,
   leaves picked
sea salt and black pepper

Place the pork in a bowl along with a glug of olive oil, the cumin seeds, paprika, honey and some salt and pepper. Massage the seasonings and honey into the pork, then leave to marinate for 2 hours.

Preheat the oven to 200°C/180°C fan/Gas Mark 6.

Transfer the pork, with the marinade, to a roasting tin and add the quince. Roast for 10 minutes, then turn down the temperature to 150°C/130°C fan/Gas Mark 2 and roast for a further 10 minutes or until the meat has caramelised but is still nice and pink inside. The quince should be just tender.

Remove the pork and quince from the tin and set aside to rest in a warm spot. Place the tin on a medium heat and add the vinegar, quince paste and stock. Bring to the boil, scraping the tin to release any sediment on the bottom. Reduce the sauce by half. Add any resting juices from the pork. Season to taste and reserve.

Slice the pork and arrange on plates with the quince. Spoon over the sweet-sour sauce and sprinkle liberally with fresh marjoram leaves. Try this dish with my Olive Oil-roasted Potatoes (see page 110).

Wood Pigeon
with Lardo, Pomegranate Molasses and Salted Walnuts

We have a bounty of year-round wood pigeon in the UK and it is to our shame that we don't eat nearly as much of this delicious, healthy meat as we should. While good restaurants have featured it for many years, it is rare to find it used to any great degree in our homes, perhaps partly due to the bird's reputation as a pest and also the unfamiliarity around cooking it.

Unlike its urban cousin, the countryside wild pigeon has a clean, varied diet of grains, peas, seeds and herbs, which means the meat has great depth of flavour. The pigeon's varied diet and busy flight style means its meat retains a naturally sweet-sour flavour.

As a lean meat it needs the addition of some fat to help keep things nice and moist. The sweet-sour marinade accentuates the natural flavour of the bird while at the same time tenderising the meat, creating a delicious glaze.

*Serves 4
as a tapas meal or
2 as a starter*

4 small oven-ready wood pigeons, spatchcocked (backbones removed and breasts flattened – your butcher will do this for you)
100ml pomegranate molasses
50ml red wine vinegar (such as cabernet sauvignon)
a small handful of rosemary leaves, finely chopped
50g walnuts
olive oil
8 thin strips of lardo (or fatty pancetta)
seeds from ½ pomegranate
sea salt and black pepper

Preheat the oven to 180°C/160°C fan/Gas Mark 4.

Lay the pigeons out skin side up on a tray. Season well and pour over the molasses and vinegar. Rub all over into the meat. Sprinkle with the rosemary, then leave the birds to marinate for an hour or so.

Meanwhile, spread the walnuts in a small baking tray and drizzle over some olive oil. Toast in the oven for 7 minutes or until fragrant and the oils have started to leach from the nuts. Remove from the oven and immediately sprinkle with plenty of sea salt. Set aside.

Heat a large sauté pan over a medium heat and add a glug of olive oil. When the oil is hot, fry the pigeons, 1 or 2 at a time, for 2 minutes on each side. Transfer to a roasting tin, placing the birds skin side up. Lay the lardo strips across the pigeon breasts. Add any marinade remaining in the tray. Roast for 8–10 minutes. Remove from the oven and leave to rest for a few minutes before serving, sprinkled with the fresh pomegranate seeds and the salted walnuts.

This is great served with a bowl of Ajo Blanco (see page 281) on the side.

Oloroso-pickled Partridge

Moorish Spain has a famously long history of pickling and preserving meats and fish. It's a method developed by the Arabs and still very much in use today. Treating lean and sometimes tough game with this method tenderises the meat and allows the game lover to enjoy this singularly seasonal meat out of season.

I use this pickling method in order to eek out a few more precious partridge pleasures over the spring and early summer months.

I've added a sweet and nutty Oloroso sherry into the pickling brine – the Oloroso's autumnal notes work really well with partridge, adding a lovely balsamic-style sweetness. The green olives add a little zip of delightful piquancy.

Serves 4

2 oven-ready grey-leg partridges
olive oil
1 carrot, peeled and finely sliced
1 large banana shallot, finely sliced
pared zest of ½ orange
1 cinnamon stick
2 star anise

100ml moscatel or chardonnay vinegar
250ml Oloroso sherry
100ml extra virgin olive oil
50g pitted green olives (such as Arbequina), cut in half, plus 100ml of the olive brine
sea salt and black pepper

Season the partridges inside and out. Set a medium flameproof casserole over a medium heat and add a good glug of olive oil. When hot, brown the partridges all over. Remove the birds from the pot and add the carrot, shallot, orange zest, cinnamon and star anise. Cook for 3 minutes to soften the vegetables.

Add the birds back to the pot. Pour over the vinegar, sherry and extra virgin olive oil and top up with about 250ml of water – the birds should be just covered. Bring slowly to the boil, then turn down the heat to a simmer. Add the olives with the brine. Cover the casserole and cook for 1 hour.

Remove from the heat, take off the lid and leave to cool.

Lift the birds out of the pot and pull off all the meat in good chunks. Place in a sterilised jar or plastic lidded container. Whisk the cooking liquor, then pour into the jar or container (including olives, vegetables and spices) to cover the partridge completely. Seal the jar or container. Leave in the fridge to pickle for at least 4 days. The pickle can be kept in the fridge for at least 2 months.

Serve at room temperature with warm bread and a fresh salad, such as my Broad Bean, Tomato and Anchovy Salad (see page 92).

FRUITS

Upon their arrival in Spain and Sicily the Moors began to plant orange trees strategically along their way as they ploughed inland – a form of both marking their new territory and also introducing an exotic new fruit to their land of occupation. It was a fruit that not only thrived but also flourished, taking to its new surroundings like a duck takes to water, happily embracing the hot summer months and the cooler, wetter winters. Oranges are now grown all year round, the more bitter Seville-style orange (the only orange for making authentic marmalade) fruiting in the winter season, the sweeter varieties becoming ready to pick over the summer months. Sicilians love using oranges in many of their dishes, sometimes whizzing them into refreshing ice-cold granitas or grating the zest onto fresh fish mixed with herbs to make a gremolata. In Spain you'll find sweet orange segments tossed into salads with salty olives and anchovies or perhaps the peeled zest used to infuse milk and cream to cook their famous arroz con leche, the delicious Spanish rice pudding.

I love the exotic fruits of Middle Eastern origin that travelled with the Moors through Europe growing in abundance along the way – truly a culinary journey of worth.

I adore the otherworldliness of figs. There is nothing that can surpass serving a just ripe fig, bursting at its seams with sweet juiciness, dressed with a sprinkle of salt, happily sitting beside a modest portion of sheep's cheese – the fig doing most of the work, delivering a sweetness, texture and jammy sauce from its juices, complementing the salty acidity of the sheep's cheese.

Quinces need to be cooked in order to be eaten. Roast or poach the fruit with some sugar and perhaps a few aromats and you are in for a treat. It is a fruit with a singular flavour, somehow ancient and earthly while at the same time honeyed and ambrosial. At its simplest, when poached with spices and sugar and served with a whipped cream, it is sublime. In Spain they make a quince 'cheese' or 'membrillo' – simply, quinces cooked down with sugar and then set with the fruit's pectin to form a jelly. You'll often find membrillo served with cheeses as a sweet accompaniment.

The arrival of the pomegranate is something to look forward to in the winter months. Once the tough skin has been penetrated you'll be rewarded inside with sweet little red gems. I'm addicted to the sweet-sour pomegranate molasses that I use for many dishes, both sweet and savoury. My recipe for a pomegranate ripple ice cream uses both fresh pomegranate and molasses and is served with a delicious pistachio turrón (see page 220).

Stone fruits, such as peaches and apricots, were already growing on the arrival of the Moors. My recipes are influenced by Arabic flavour combinations and techniques. One of the finest things I've eaten in recent years was in Sicily where a pristine white peach was cut and lightly grilled, the smokiness contrasting beautifully with the sweet juicy peach, adding a little caramelised texture . Served with a little splash of rose water it transported me to another imagined far off world of sultans and long lost Arabian nights.

Almond Granita
with Roasted Grapes

Granitas are a specialty of Sicily and one of the glories of the Moorish legacy. A granita is a simple mixture of water and sugar with a flavouring that is then frozen and scraped with a fork to form a delicious, refreshing 'snow'.

On a trip to Palermo I stayed in a very swish hotel where part of the breakfast buffet consisted of a granita bar. Each morning I was confronted with a glistening row of sliver canisters filled with all the flavours of the culinary rainbow – almond, coffee, orange, lemon – all available to mix and match. And then, just to add to the gastronomic extravaganza, there was a multitude of wonderful toppings from which to choose – fruits, nuts, whipped cream... I was like the proverbial kid in a sweet shop, unfailingly pitching up each morning, shamelessly compiling indulgent iced mixes and topping marriages.

This is my version of the granita extravaganza which I like to serve in an iced glass, making for a wonderfully refreshing and satisfying finish to a long and lovely summer lunch. Should the mood take you then you could serve your granita in a warm brioche for a truly indulgent finish.

Grinding your own almonds makes all the difference ensuring that you retain all the wonderful fresh, natural almond oils.

Serves 6

200g blanched almonds
300g caster sugar

150g black seedless grapes
50ml runny honey

Grind the almonds to a powder in a food processor.

Pour 1 litre of water into a saucepan and add the sugar. Bring to the boil, stirring to dissolve the sugar, then simmer slowly for 7 minutes. Transfer the syrup to a bowl and leave to cool. When cool stir in the almonds. Chill in the fridge for at least 4 hours or overnight.

Strain the almond syrup through a sieve and discard the almonds. Pour the syrup into a freezerproof container and place in the freezer – every hour scrape through the mixture with a fork until it has frozen all the way through and resembles snow.

Preheat the oven to 190°C/170°C fan/Gas Mark 5. Cut the grapes in half lengthways and spread on a baking tray cut side up. Drizzle over the honey. Roast the grapes for 20 minutes or until the juices start to bleed and the skins lightly blister. Cool.

Serve the grapes at room temperature with the granita.

Left: Grilled Peaches with Rose Water and Buttermilk Panna Cotta (see page 213)
Top right: Rose-scented Meringues with Roasted Cherries and Ginjinah (see page 212)
Bottom right: Almond Granita with Roasted Grapes (see page 209)

Rose-scented Meringues
with Roasted Cherries and Ginjinah

This is such a pretty dessert, all shades of pinks and reds, and though it looks rather decadent it's actually quite light and fresh.

Rose water is a popular ingredient throughout the Middle East, where it was first distilled to add to perfumes. Now it's prominent in many sweets, teas, pastries and dairy products. It needs to be used sparingly otherwise it can overpower!

Ginjinah is a very popular Portuguese sour cherry liqueur. If you struggle to find it you can substitute with any cherry liquor.

Serves 4

150g pitted fresh cherries
120g caster sugar
125ml Ginjinha or other
    cherry liqueur
120ml double cream
80ml thick Greek yoghurt
dried rose petals, to
    decorate (optional)

Meringues
unsalted butter, for greasing
4 egg whites
200g caster sugar
1 teaspoon rose water

First make the meringues. Preheat the oven to 130°C/110°C fan/Gas Mark ¾. Grease a baking tray and line with baking parchment.

Whisk the egg whites in a free-standing electric mixer, or with a hand-held electric mixer, on maximum speed. When they are frothy, gradually whisk in the sugar and keep whisking until the mixture doubles in volume to make a stiff and glossy meringue. Whisk in the rose water.

Spoon the meringue mix on to the prepared baking tray in rounds about 10cm in diameter. You should be able to make 8 meringues. Place in the oven and cook for 1 hour. Turn off the oven but do not open the oven door for another hour – doing this means you will have beautiful meringues that are crisp on the outside and soft and chewy within. Set them aside.

Turn the oven on again, to heat to 180°C/160°C fan/Gas Mark 4.

Place the cherries and 60g of the sugar in a small baking dish. Roast for 20 minutes or until the cherries begin to caramelise and release their juices. Add the liqueur and 50ml of water and stir to mix, then roast for a further 10 minutes or until the liquid has reduced and turned syrupy. Remove from the oven and reserve.

Whip the cream in a bowl to the soft peak stage. Add the remaining sugar and whisk in, then mix in the yoghurt.

To serve, sandwich the cream and cherries between pairs of meringues and drizzle over the cherry liqueur syrup. Scatter over some dried rose petals, if using.

Grilled Peaches
with Rose Water and Buttermilk Panna Cotta

I love the contrast of the bitterness of the charred peaches when set against the natural sweetness of their flesh.

Charring can be a great solution to the problem of slightly underripe stone fruit badly in need of a little cooking to coax out the sweet, syrupy juices from within. On the flip side very ripe fruit should never be charred as they will almost certainly turn to mush.

The rose water and buttermilk work harmoniously in the very lightly set, wobbly panna cotta – the buttermilk adding a refreshing, slightly acidic tang and the rose water working its sultry exoticness. I like to serve this dessert in early summer.

Serves 4

2 large, quite firm yellow peaches,
   cut in half and stone removed
caster sugar, to dust the fruits

Panna cotta
2 sheets/leaves gelatine

300ml double cream
70g caster sugar
3 drops of rose water
300ml buttermilk

To make the panna cotta, soak the gelatine in cold water to soften it. Bring the cream and sugar slowly to the boil in a saucepan, then remove from the heat. Drain the gelatine and squeeze out excess water, then whisk into the cream until completely melted. Add the rose water and whisk in the buttermilk.

Pour the mix into 4 small pudding moulds and place in the fridge. Leave for at least 2 hours to set.

Prepare and light a charcoal fire in a barbecue – the coals should burn down to an ashen grey before cooking. Alternatively, heat a ridged grill pan over a medium hob heat.

Press the cut side of the peach halves into caster sugar to coat, then place them on the barbecue grill or hot pan. Cook for 4–5 minutes or until nicely caramelised. Turn the peach halves over and cook for a further 2–3 minutes or until the fruit has slightly softened and is lightly singed at the edges.

Remove the peaches from the barbecue or pan and rest for a minute or so. Meanwhile, dip the panna cotta moulds in hot water, then turn out the panna cotta on to plates – they will be quite soft. Serve with a peach half on the side.

Caramelised Fig Tart
with Muscovado Sugar and Goat's Milk

The fig is the fruit that best epitomises the rich culinary culture of both the Middle East and also the Mediterranean – exotic, sensual, delicious and other worldly.

Wonderful on its own but when baked into this syrupy, tatin-style tart the fig becomes something else altogether, the natural sugars mixing sublimely with the complex muscovado caramel.

Best-quality, shop-bought puff pastry is perfectly acceptable for this dish but ensure that you buy the all-butter variety. I love the flavour of full cream goat's milk – the saltiness and tang of the cheese sits so well with the rich, sweet figs.

Serves 6

30g cold unsalted butter
110g muscovado sugar
6 black figs (ripe but not over ripe and broken)
1 cinnamon stick

grated zest of 1 lemon
100ml full-cream goat's milk
100ml goat's cream
1 x 275g roll all-butter puff pastry
1 egg yolk beaten with a little milk

Preheat the oven to 180°C/160°C fan/Gas Mark 4.

You need a medium-size non-stick, ovenproof sauté pan. Slice the butter thinly and lay over the bottom of the pan. Sprinkle over 80g of the sugar. Cut the figs in half and place them cut side down, in one layer, over the sugar. Press them down a little so they are snug. Insert the cinnamon stick between the figs and grate over the lemon zest.

Put the milk, cream and the rest of the sugar in a saucepan. Bring to the boil, stirring to dissolve the sugar, then reduce by about half until thick and almost custard-like. Set aside to cool to room temperature.

Roll out the puff pastry on a floured surface into a rough round about 3mm thick and 5cm wider than the pan. Transfer to a tray lined with baking parchment. Prick the pastry all over with a fork, then place in the fridge.

Set the pan with the figs on a medium heat. Cook for about 8 minutes or until the sugar and butter have melted and turned a dark caramel colour and the figs have just started to bleed. Remove the pan from the heat and cool for 5 minutes.

Lay the pastry round over the figs and push the pastry edges down between the side of the pan and the figs. Brush the pastry lid with the egg yolk wash. Place the pan in the oven and bake for 20 minutes or until the pastry is crisp and a deep golden brown.

Remove from the oven and cool for 5 minutes before flipping out on to a plate. Serve hot with the reduced creamy milk.

Torrijas (Eggy Bread)
with Sticky Dates

This is one of my all-time favourite desserts. It's fantastically indulgent and so I like to serve it around Christmas time – the cinnamon and dried, candied fruit flavours seem just right for the season. In essence this is a deluxe version of French toast but using a spiced fruit bread (panettone is best for this) bound with a rich custard, then frozen and finally fried like a doughnut. It's very easy to prepare and can be mostly made in advance ahead of the final frying.

It's incredible served with sticky dates in their own syrup. Dates are widely associated with the Middle East where they are grown and eaten in abundance but they can also be found in the warmer pockets of Andalucía such as in Iznájar where the Moors planted date palms during their occupation. Hunt out Medjool dates, often known as toffee dates, which are the best variety and have the most incredible caramel flavour once dried.

Serves 4–6

1kg panettone or other brioche-style fruit bread, trimmed and cut into slices
12 Medjool dates, stones removed
75ml date syrup
1.5 litres vegetable oil, for deep-frying
40g caster sugar

20g ground cinnamon
plain flour, for dusting

Custard
375ml double cream
375ml full-cream milk
3 egg yolks
50g muscovado sugar

For the custard, bring the cream and milk to the boil in a medium saucepan. Whisk the egg yolks and sugar together in a bowl, then add a little of the hot milk/cream mix and stir in. Pour this mix into the simmering milk/cream mix in the pan and cook slowly, stirring constantly, until just thickened enough to coat the back of the spoon. Immediately take the custard off the heat and pour into a bowl to cool.

Line a plastic container or tray, such as an ice cream tub, with baking parchment (the container needs to be big enough to fit in all the bread and custard, in a depth of 3–4cm). Make layers of panettone in the container, coating each layer with custard. Cover with a sheet of baking parchment and press the panettone down firmly. Freeze overnight to form an ice cream-panettone 'block'.

Remove from the freezer and thaw slightly before quickly cutting into 8 slices (4 portions). Place these torrijas back in the freezer and leave there until ready to fry.

Put the dates in a small pan with the syrup. Bring to the boil and boil for 2 minutes to reduce the syrup by a third. Set aside.

Heat the oil in a large, deep pan to about 170°C. Mix together the sugar and cinnamon on a plate. Toss the frozen torrijas in flour, then deep-fry for a few minutes until golden brown on both sides. Drain on kitchen paper, then transfer to the cinnamon sugar and turn to coat before serving hot, with the dates and syrup on the side.

Poached Apricots
with Orange Flower Water and Whipped Mascarpone

The origin of the apricot is shrouded in mystery and uncertainty. Said by some to have originated in Armenia, others that its beginnings lay in the Far East. We do know that they've been cultivated in Persia since antiquity and from there spread through Europe where they grow abundantly in Spain and the southern parts of Italy in particular. Apricots were and still are an important fruit in Arabic and Moorish cuisine.

Delicious and versatile when fresh, they also dry and preserve well. When dried they have an intense sweet-sour flavour and are used to brilliant effect when added to tagines and sauces to give depth of flavour. I've used both fresh and dried in this recipe, the textures contrasting well together.

Serves 4

75g golden caster sugar
pared zest of ½ orange
6 dried apricots (an organic
    variety is best as they don't
    include preservatives)

6 fresh apricots, cut in half and
    stone removed
5 drops of orange flower water
100ml full-fat mascarpone
seeds from ½ vanilla pod

Place 50g of the sugar and 150ml of water in a saucepan with the orange zest and slowly bring to a simmer. Add the dried apricots and cook for 3 minutes. Add the fresh apricot halves and continue to cook for 10 minutes or until the fruits are tender and the liquid has turned syrupy.

Remove from the heat. Stir in the flower water and leave to macerate for at least 1 hour at room temperature.

Vigorously whisk the mascarpone with the remaining sugar and the vanilla seeds until fully incorporated.

Serve the poached apricots and some syrup with dollops of mascarpone. This is also delicious with my almond and caramel ice cream (see page 222).

Pistachio and Sesame Turrón
with Pomegranate Ripple Ice Cream

The origins of turrón were thought to have come about in the 10th century when the Muslim conquest was in full swing and there was much movement of their armies. A transportable, nutrient-rich food source was needed that wouldn't spoil on long, hot marches. There are many variations of the cooked honey/nut combinations all over Spain. This version is a hard, brittle type as opposed to the very soft and chewy versions found further east. This turrón goes well with the pomegranate ripple ice cream here but is also great on its own with coffee.

Serves 8–10

Turrón
2 egg whites
200g caster sugar
350g runny honey
450g toasted almonds
100g green pistachios (ideally Iranian)
100g sesame seeds
4 drops of anise extract

Ice cream
300ml full-cream milk
200ml double cream
100g caster sugar
4 egg yolks
75ml thick pomegranate molasses

Whisk the egg whites in a bowl until they form stiff peaks. Heat the caster sugar with 3 tablespoons of water until you achieve a clear syrup. Remove from the heat. In another pan heat the honey until it liquifies. Add to the sugar syrup. Put the syrup-honey mix back on the heat and cook until it turns a dark golden-brown colour (known as the hard ball stage). Remove from the heat and add the almonds, pistachios and sesame seeds along with the anise and egg whites. Mix well to ensure there are no egg white lumps in the mix, which will take a few minutes.

Line a 15 x 20cm rectangular baking tin with baking parchment. Pour the mix into the tin and smooth out with a spatula. Place another piece of parchment on top and then a wooden board or thick card that fits into the tin to weight the mix (if using card, set some weight on it such as 2 or 3 cans of food). Place in the fridge and leave for at least 2 days to set.

To make the ice cream, heat the milk and double cream to a simmer. Whisk together the sugar and egg yolks in a bowl until pale and light. Add a few splashes of the hot cream mix to the eggs and whisk well, then add this mixture to the hot cream in the pan. Cook slowly over a low heat, stirring constantly, until the mixture starts to thicken to a custard that will coat the back of the spoon. Immediately remove from the heat and pour the custard into a container to cool. Once cooled, chill well.

Churn the custard in an ice cream machine until nearly set. Transfer to a freezerproof container. Stir in the molasses to form ripples. Freeze for at least 2 hours before serving.

Uncover the turrón and turn out on to a board. Peel off the baking parchment from the base. The turrón will still be slightly wet, which is normal for a fresh, home-made version and is all the more delicious for it. Cut the turrón into chunks and serve with scoops of the ice cream, or on its own sprinkled with icing sugar.

Slow-cooked Quince
with Oloroso and Salted Almond Caramel Ice Cream

The quince is my favourite winter fruit by far. It looks like a cross between an apple and a pear but rather more knobbly and misshapen. It's a fruit that when cooked with love and care will reward with the most sublime, honeyed, sweet-sour flavours.

Oloroso is a variety of sherry produced in Jerez in Andalucía. It is deep, rich, complex and dark (though to a lesser degree than the Christmas pudding-like Pedro Ximinez) but with a fresh citrus note on the finish – it's well worth hunting out.

I also love to serve quinces with fatty, salty meats to add a sweet contrast.

Serves 4–5

200g caster sugar
200ml Oloroso sherry
grated zest and juice of 1 lemon
1 star anise
1 cinnamon stick
4 medium quinces

Ice cream
340g caster sugar
450ml double cream
300ml semi-skimmed milk
8 egg yolks
½ teaspoon almond essence
½ teaspoon Maldon sea salt

First make the ice cream. Place a pan on the hob to heat. Once hot, put 280g of the caster sugar into the pan and heat, shaking the pan occasionally, until the sugar melts and turns a good caramel colour. Add the double cream, stir and bring to the boil. Add the milk.

Meanwhile, beat the egg yolks with the remaining caster sugar in a bowl until pale, light and fluffy. Very slowly pour the hot caramel cream on to the yolks while whisking. Strain into a bowl and cool, then chill well.

Stir the almond essence and salt into the chilled mixture. Churn in an ice cream machine, then transfer to a freezerproof container and place in the freezer. (The ice cream will serve more than 4–5, but the excess can be kept in the freezer to enjoy another time.)

For the quince, put the sugar, Oloroso, lemon zest, spices and 200ml of water in a medium saucepan and bring slowly to the boil. Meanwhile, peel the quinces and cut in half lengthways, then rub with the lemon juice to prevent them from oxidising.

When the poaching liquor starts boiling, add the quinces and turn down to a simmer. Place a piece of baking parchment on top and poach gently for 1 hour 20 minutes or until the quinces have turned a deep amber and are beautifully soft.

Using a slotted spoon, transfer the quinces to a plate and leave to cool. Turn up the heat and boil the poaching liquor to reduce to a syrupy consistency. Strain through a sieve into a bowl and cool.

Cut the cooled quinces in half again lengthways and remove the core. Place the quince pieces back in the syrup and leave to macerate for at least an hour. Serve the quinces at room temperature with scoops of salted almond caramel ice cream.

Blood Orange and Saffron Jelly
with Blood Orange Granita

This recipe is a love letter to the blood orange. The blood orange, a slightly bittersweet citrus fruit, is only available in the winter months after Christmas. Aside from the delicious flavour of the blood orange itself, which I absolutely love, it is also the crazy colouring of the flesh that gets me excited.

The colours of the blood orange rainbow are an intoxicating swirl of yellow, orange, pink, purple and red, offering the willing participant a gastronomic, psychedelic freak-out.

It's a culinary trip well worth taking!

Serves 6–8

Jelly
700ml blood orange juice (from
   9–10 oranges)
175g caster sugar
½ teaspoon saffron threads
7 small sheets/leaves of gelatine
   (14g in total)

Granita
220g caster sugar
500ml blood orange juice (from
   7–8 oranges)

For the jelly, pour the orange juice into a saucepan and add the sugar and saffron threads. Place over a medium heat, whisking to dissolve the sugar. Meanwhile, soak the gelatine in cold water to soften it. Drain the gelatine and squeeze out excess water, then whisk into the hot juice until completely melted.

Strain the mix through a sieve and pour into individual glasses or a large serving bowl. Cover and place in the fridge. Leave to set for about 4 hours.

For the granita, put the sugar and 300ml of water into a saucepan. Bring to the boil, stirring to dissolve the sugar, then boil over a high heat to create a sugar syrup. Whisk in the blood orange juice. Pour the mix into a bowl and set aside to cool down.

Once cold, pour the syrup into a freezerproof container and freeze, every hour scraping through with a fork until the syrup is completely frozen and resembles snow.

Serve the jelly alongside the granita for an incredibly fresh and light finish to a dinner.

Arroz con Leche
with Salted Caramel Pears and Raisins

The delicious sweet rice puddings of the Middle East were clearly an influence on the Spanish arroz con leche, which are typically flavoured with cinnamon and citrus zest. The early rice dishes would have been sweetened with raw honey and infused with rose water.

A short-grain rice is essential for a successful rice pudding as it both absorbs the rich milk and aromats and also releases its starch to help thicken the pudding, making it gloriously creamy and rich. The Spaniards use their Bomba rice, the rice of paella, but risotto rice works just as well.

Please don't skimp on the milk – if you use a good-quality full-cream milk it will pay back with huge flavour dividends for this most comforting of puddings.

Serves 6

Rice pudding
250g short-grain rice
200g caster sugar
100g raisins
850ml full-cream milk
1 vanilla pod, split open lengthways
1 cinnamon stick
grated zest of 1 lemon

Pears
100g caster sugar
20g unsalted butter
60ml double cream
½ teaspoon sea salt
2 ripe Comice or Packham pears, peeled, cored and cut into 6 lengthways

Put all the ingredients for the rice pudding in a medium saucepan. Bring to the boil, then turn down to a simmer and cook for about 1 hour or until the rice is tender and the milk has reduced to a rich creamy consistency.

While the pudding cooks get the pears ready. Heat a medium sauté pan over a low heat. Add the sugar and butter and cook slowly, without stirring, to create a dark golden caramel. Immediately add the cream (be careful as it will spit) and stir into the caramel, then add the salt and pears. Cook over the lowest heat for 2–3 minutes, turning the pears several times, until they are quite tender and coated with caramel.

Serve the rice pudding in bowls topped with pieces of pear and then the caramel.

SWEET BAKING

Nowhere is the Moorish influence felt more than in the sugar-laden bakes, pastries, fritters and tarts of the region. It was the Moors who introduced the world to the delights and endless possibilities of sugar cane and the means to refine it to caster, icing, granulated and brown sugars.

Fried sweet pastries such as the Sicilian cannoli (usually stuffed with whipped ricotta and cream, see page 250) have deep Arabic origins. These were simple rough pastries traditionally fried in hot oil and then sweetened with raw honey for a filling, sweet treat. The natural refinement of sugar cane has shaped these modern versions but their roots in Arabia are still clear to see.

I love the use of the ultra sweet candied fruits found in Sicilian markets, which are lovingly baked or whipped into their desserts. If you've been to Sicily you'll have seen market vendors with baskets of multi-coloured dried fruit slices preserved with sugar syrups – delicious, tooth-numbingly sweet treats, to be eaten either on their own or diced and mixed into delicious desserts such as the Cassata Siciliana (see page 245). The Arabs originally preserved fruits in honey or palm oil to prolong their shelf life. Soon they became a focal point for important feasts and banquets when they were presented to honoured guests. Candied fruits are widely available and I recommend going as colourful as the selection will allow!

I've included some very traditional desserts and cakes in this section but also added some of my own that encapsulate my love of these sweet, irresistible flavours.

Polvorón (Mantecado)

A complex and interesting story belies these simple but pleasant biscuits. The biscuits were originally bought to Andalucía by the Moors (their origins before that stemmed from the Levant, with a very similar sweet known as ghurayba) during the occupation.

In 1478 at the Spanish Inquisition, it was decreed that the popular polvorones were to be made using pork fat so as to weed out any secret Arabs or Jews in southern Spain! (Mantecado refers to a variety of shortbreads that have pork lard as the fat medium.)

These biscuits are quite short in texture and have a lovely smokiness to them from the roasted flour process – traditionally they are served around Christmas time but often eaten all-year round nowadays.

Makes 24–26

800g plain flour, sifted, plus extra
　for dusting
400g lard
200g ground almonds

375g icing sugar, plus extra for dusting
1 teaspoon ground cinnamon
2 teaspoons sesame seeds,
　for sprinkling

Heat the grill to 200°C or medium-high.

Sift the flour on to a baking tray and toast under the grill until the top layer becomes golden brown. Remove from the grill and stir to mix the browned flour into the white flour, then toast again. Repeat this process 4 or 5 times until all the flour has been toasted to golden brown. Set aside to cool.

Melt a large knob of the lard in a sauté pan over a low heat and lightly fry the ground almonds until they are a light golden brown. Remove from the heat and cool.

Once the flour and nuts have cooled, mix together all of the ingredients (except the sesame seeds), making sure to incorporate all of the lard. The dough should come together when you press on it, but also should easily fall apart. You may need to add a little more lard to achieve the right texture. Wrap the dough in clingfilm and chill for 20 minutes.

Preheat the oven to 180°C/160°C fan/Gas Mark 4.

Roll out the dough on a floured surface until about 1cm thick. Using a 3cm round pastry cutter, cut out discs and lay them on a baking tray. Sprinkle on the sesame seeds. Bake for 12–14 minutes or until the biscuits turn a light golden brown.

Remove from the oven and sprinkle with the extra icing sugar, then leave to cool fully before eating. Traditionally these are served in twisted waxed paper, like a classic sweet. I've done this and given them as a gift.

Seville Orange Tart
with Bitter Chocolate Ganache

Seville oranges are around in the winter months of January and February – I've always thought of this as a present from nature, to have such lovely, vibrant citruses at the most cold and depressing time of year.

Seville oranges are a bitter orange variety and are usually used for a classic marmalade recipe, of which I'm a huge fan.

This tart has a slightly bitter note but all the more delicious and interesting for it. The hit of dark chocolate is an added bonus to this stunner of a tart.

Serves 8

Pastry
175g plain flour, plus extra for dusting
50g icing sugar
a pinch of salt
100g chilled unsalted butter, cut into cubes
grated zest of 1 small orange (not Seville)
1 free-range egg, separated
2 teaspoons orange juice

Tart filling
4 Seville oranges (or blood oranges)
6 free-range eggs
250g caster sugar
150ml double cream

Ganache
150ml double cream
150g dark chocolate (70% cocoa solids), chopped

First make the pastry. Sift the flour, sugar and salt into a food processor and pulse to mix. With the machine running, add the butter and orange zest and blitz until you have a mixture that resembles breadcrumbs. Tip into a bowl and stir in the egg yolk and orange juice to bring together into a dough. Knead briefly until smooth, then set aside in the fridge to rest for 30 minutes.

Roll out the pastry dough on a floured surface and use to line a greased 23cm round, loose-bottomed tart tin that is 4cm deep. Prick the pastry base with a fork. Chill for 20 minutes.

Preheat the oven to 180°C/160°C fan/Gas Mark 4.

Line the pastry case with a sheet of baking parchment and fill with baking beans or rice. Bake blind for 15 minutes or until the edges of the pastry start to brown. Remove the paper and beans and bake for a further 5 minutes or until the base is crisp and lightly coloured.

Whisk the egg white until frothy, then brush all over the inside of the pastry case. Bake for 2 minutes to seal. Remove from the oven to cool. Turn the oven down to 110°C/90°C fan/Gas Mark ¼.

For the tart filling, grate the orange zest and reserve. Squeeze the juice from the oranges through a sieve; reserve the juice.

Whisk together the eggs and sugar in a bowl until pale and light but not frothy. Add the orange juice and cream, and whisk well to incorporate. Whisk in the zest. Transfer to a jug.

Partially pull out an oven shelf and place the tart case on it. Pour in the orange custard, then carefully push the shelf back into the oven. Bake for 45 minutes or until the custard has started to set but is still wobbly in the centre. Remove from the oven and cool for at least 4 hours before removing the base of the tin and sliding the tart on to a plate.

Make the ganache while the tart is baking. Gently heat the cream in a small pan, then whisk in the chocolate until melted – don't boil. When smoothly blended, transfer to a container and leave to cool at room temperature.

To serve, cut wedges from the tart and dollop a spoonful of ganache on the side.

Top left: Semolina, Lemon Syrup and Pistachio Cake (see page 236)
Bottom left: Chestnut, Chocolate and Cinnamon Cake (see page 237)
Right: Seville Orange Tart with Bitter Chocolate Ganache (see page 232)

Semolina, Lemon Syrup and Pistachio Cake

Semolina is a by-product of the milling of durum wheat flour and has been used throughout the Middle East and North Africa for centuries in cakes, biscuits, bread and cous cous (a precursor to what we now know as pasta). Spain and in particular Sicily and southern Italy use semolina in breads and types of pastas and gnocchis.

I love the grainy, rustic texture you get when baking semolina in cakes, however, it has a tendency sometimes to be a little on the dry side, so drenching it as it comes out of the oven in a hot sweet-sour sticky lemon syrup moistens it deliciously.

The pistachios share a starring role in the cake and the bright green nuts bake down into an almost buttery-like texture.

I like to serve this cake with some extra thick yoghurt or buttermilk on the side.

Serves 8–10

150g unsalted butter, at room temperature, plus extra for greasing
150g plain flour, sifted, plus extra for dusting
160g green pistachios (preferably Iranian), plus extra chopped pistachios for decorating
90g fine semolina flour
2 heaped teaspoons baking powder

155g caster sugar
3 free-range eggs
130g thick Greek yoghurt

Syrup
215g caster sugar
grated zest and juice of 2 large unwaxed lemons

First make the syrup. Put the caster sugar, lemon zest and juice into a small saucepan, along with 200ml of water. Stir over a medium heat until the sugar dissolves. Increase the heat to high and bring to the boil, then simmer for 2 minutes or until the syrup thickens. Set aside to cool.

Preheat the oven to 180°C/160°C fan/Gas Mark 4. Brush a 20cm round non-stick cake tin with butter and dust with flour, knocking out any excess.

Blitz the pistachios in a food processor until finely ground. Sift the flour, semolina flour and baking powder into a bowl. Stir in the ground pistachios.

Using a hand-held electric mixer, beat the butter with the sugar in a separate bowl until pale and creamy. Add the eggs, one at a time, beating well after each addition. Add to the flour mixture along with the yoghurt and stir until fully combined.

Spoon the mixture into the prepared tin and smooth the surface. Bake for 50 minutes or until a skewer inserted into the centre comes out clean. Set the tin on a wire rack and use the skewer to pierce holes all over the surface of the cake. Pour the syrup over the cake. Set aside to cool.

Transfer the cake to a serving plate. Sprinkle with chopped pistachios and serve.

Chestnut, Chocolate and Cinnamon Cake

I love this indulgent, autumnal cake. It's robust and full of earthiness and nuttiness while the bitter chocolate and chestnut combination is a revelation if you've not experienced it before.

This is a cake for adults, to be eaten alongside a strong, dark cup of coffee or a glass of chilled, sticky PX sherry – or both.

Serves 8–10

175g unsalted butter, plus extra
    for the tin
175g caster sugar
325g dark chocolate, broken
    into pieces
50ml strong black coffee
70g walnut halves
85g blanched almonds

5 large free-range eggs, separated
40g vacuum-packed cooked chestnuts,
    cut into chunks
grated zest of 1 large orange
½ teaspoon ground cinnamon
80g thick, full-fat plain yoghurt
50g plain flour
icing sugar, for dusting

Preheat the oven to 180°C/160°C fan/Gas Mark 4 and butter a 20cm round springform cake tin.

Melt the butter with the caster sugar in a large heatproof bowl set over a pan of simmering water. Add the chocolate and melt it in the warm butter and sugar mixture, stirring. Stir in the coffee. Remove from the heat and cool slightly.

Toast the walnuts and blanched almonds in a dry pan, taking care they don't burn. Break up the nuts very roughly – you want a mixture of large and smaller chunks, not chopped nuts.

Add the egg yolks to the chocolate mixture along with the toasted nuts, chestnuts, orange zest, cinnamon and yoghurt and mix well. In a separate bowl, whisk the egg whites until stiff but not dry. Loosen the chocolate mixture by folding in a large spoonful of egg white, then carefully fold in the rest, along with the flour. Mix lightly so that you don't knock out the air. Pour into the prepared tin. Bake for 45 minutes or until a skewer inserted into the centre comes out clean.

Leave the cake to cool in the tin for 20 minutes, then unclasp the spring-surround and remove the cake from the base. This is quite a fragile cake, with a mousse-like middle, so handle it carefully. Set it on a wire rack to finish cooling. The top will deflate and crack a little as the cake cools.

Dust the cake with icing sugar. Alternatively, if you want a shiny finish, melt some dark chocolate in a heatproof bowl set over a pan of simmering water. Spread the melted chocolate over the top of the cake and leave to set. Roughly chop some hazelnuts and walnuts, and scatter on top.

Fig and Almond Greixonera

Greixonera is a traditional Balearic sweet bread-based pudding. Packed with fruits, nuts and spice it's delicious and comforting. I vary the fruits according to the season; cherries work well in the summer as do chunks of apples and pears in the autumn months. My favourite, however, is with ripe black figs, their sticky juices bursting into the custard creating pink trails.

The pudding is best eaten at room temperature, after it has cooled and the flavours have developed.

Serves 6–8

unsalted butter, for greasing the dish
500g day-old white bread, crusts
    removed, torn into small chunks
150g very ripe figs, each cut into 6
    pieces lengthways
25g toasted slivered almonds
500ml full-cream milk
500ml single cream
220g caster sugar

1 cinnamon stick
2 cardamom pods, crushed
pared zest of 1 unwaxed lemon
pared zest of 1 orange
6 free-range eggs
2 tablespoons sweet sherry (such
    as Oloroso)
½ teaspoon salt
60g muscovado sugar

Butter a 24cm diameter baking dish or pie dish that is 6cm deep. Lay the bread pieces in the dish and scatter over the fig pieces and half the almonds.

Put the milk, cream, caster sugar, cinnamon, cardamom and zests into a saucepan and bring to the boil. Simmer for 5 minutes. Remove from the heat and leave to infuse for 15 minutes. Strain through a sieve into a bowl and leave to cool.

In a separate bowl, whisk together the eggs, sherry and salt to combine. Whisk into the cooled milk. Pour this mix over the bread. Cover the dish and place in the fridge to soak for 4 hours or overnight.

Preheat the oven to 170°C/150°C fan/Gas Mark 3½.

Sprinkle the remaining almonds and muscovado sugar over the top of the pudding. Bake for 45 minutes or until the top is golden brown and a skewer inserted into the pudding comes out dry. Leave to cool and serve warm or at room temperature.

Churros
with Cinnamon, Hot Chocolate Sauce and Whipped Cream

Churros are thought to have originated in Portugal during the Moorish occupation when spices and other produce were being introduced. These fantastic doughnuts are a close relative of the Moroccan street food favourite *sfenj*.

Ubiquitous across Spain you will find them in various guises, for example the Andalucíans call their version calientes and are coiled, fried and sliced like a cake. They are consumed *en masse* for breakfast, washed down with a super strong coffee or sweet hot chocolate (the Spanish know a healthy breakfast).

I could eat these fried, hot delights all day long – the cinnamon, chocolate and orange triumvirate is an absolute winner. If you intend to make these regularly you should probably invest in a churros-maker or *churrera* available from homeware stores or online.

Makes about 24 to serve 5–6

120g plain flour, sifted
120g self-raising flour, sifted
a pinch of salt
400ml boiling water
grated zest of ½ orange
2 tablespoons extra virgin olive oil
vegetable oil, for frying
180g caster sugar
2 tablespoons ground cinnamon

200ml double cream, whipped to soft peaks

Chocolate sauce
200ml full-cream milk
40g unsalted butter
300g bitter dark chocolate (with 70% cocoa solids)

Mix together both the flours and the salt in a large mixing bowl. In a separate bowl whisk together the boiling water, orange zest and olive oil. Pour the water/oil mix on to the flour and stir with a spoon for a minute or so until the mix comes together to make a soft, sticky dough. Leave to rest for 30 minutes before using.

For the chocolate sauce, heat the milk in a saucepan over a medium heat until hot. Add the butter and chocolate and stir over the heat until the chocolate and butter have melted and the sauce is rich and glossy. Remove from the heat and keep warm.

Smear a tray with vegetable oil. Put the dough into a *churrera*/churros-maker or a piping bag fitted with a star nozzle and pipe out 12–15cm long doughnuts on to the oiled tray. Coil them into spirals for a hybrid churros/calientes.

Heat the vegetable oil in a deep pan or deep-fat fryer to 170°C. Mix together the caster sugar and cinnamon in a bowl, ready to coat the churros.

Carefully fry the churros, in batches, for about 3 minutes, then turn them over and fry for a further 2 minutes or until they are golden brown all over. Remove with a slotted spoon and drain well on kitchen paper, then toss through the cinnamon sugar while still hot, so the sugar sticks. Serve with the warm chocolate sauce and whipped cream on the side.

Cardamom Biscuit
with Intense Bitter Chocolate Ice Cream and PX Raisin Syrup

While chocolate may not have Arabic origins, the complex flavours of bitter chocolate evoke the heady, sultry flavours of Moorish cuisine.

This ice cream is, as the title says, *intense*; I'd go as far as to say perhaps the most bitter, chocolaty ice cream I've tasted simply due to the extra high chocolate content and the addition of some coffee to accentuate the bitter-sweet flavour. Spices, citrus and mulled fruits all come into it with the Pedro Ximenez and biscuit.

The recipe will make more ice cream than is required but it will keep in the freezer for up to three months.

Serves 10–12

Bitter chocolate ice cream
500ml full-cream milk
100g cocoa powder
100g caster sugar
100g dark chocolate (70% cocoa solids)
50ml strong espresso coffee
3g glucose

PX raisin syrup
100g raisins
200ml Pedro Ximinez sherry

Cardamom biscuits
4 cardamom pods
160g plain flour, sifted, plus extra for dusting
20g icing sugar
a pinch of salt
110g unsalted butter

First make the ice cream. Bring the milk to a simmer in a saucepan and whisk in the cocoa powder and sugar until fully dissolved. Remove from the heat and reserve.

Put the chocolate, coffee and glucose in the top of a bain-marie, or heatproof bowl, and slowly melt over simmering water. Whisk this into the milk mixture. Allow to cool completely, then churn in an ice cream machine. Transfer to a freezerproof container and freeze for at least 4 hours before serving.

Alternatively, you can make this without an ice cream machine. Put the mix in a freezerproof container and place in the freezer, then whisk the mix every 30 minutes for 3 hours or so to break up the ice crystals as they form. This method will work well although the result won't be as smooth as with an ice cream machine.

For the syrup, put the raisins and sherry in a saucepan, bring to a simmer and cook gently for 5 minutes to soften the raisins and slightly reduce the sherry to a syrup. Remove from the heat and reserve.

...continued on page 244

To make the biscuits, crush the cardamom pods and put the seeds into a mortar. Grind with the pestle until fine. Tip into a bowl and add the flour, icing sugar and salt. Add the butter and rub in with your fingertips until the mix resembles fine breadcrumbs.

Turn the mix out on to a floured surface and work quickly with your hands to make a smooth dough. Divide the dough in half and shape each into a 'log'. Wrap in clingfilm and chill for an hour.

Preheat the oven to 160°C/140°C fan/Gas Mark 3.

Remove the logs of dough from the fridge and slice them into 1cm rounds. Lay these side by side on a non-stick baking tray. Bake for 20 minutes or until a light golden brown. Cool on a wire rack.

To serve, put scoops of the chocolate ice cream into serving dishes and spoon over the PX raisin syrup. Either crumble the cardamom biscuits on top or serve them on the side for dipping.

Cassata Siciliana

This is a real show stopper of a cake – a Sicilian classic that's as delicious as it is garish with its jewel-like candied fruits. The early versions of this cake were first made in Palermo around the 10th century during the Muslim occupation. The Arabic word *qas'ah*, from which cassata has derived, refers to the bowl that the cake is traditionally shaped in.

As this cake is all about the candied fruits it's worth taking your time to get some really top-notch ones. The best candied fruits will be sweet but with a subtle taste of their natural flavour: buywholefoodsonline.co.uk stock some lovely whole fruits and they are all natural and organic.

This cake is meant to be a beautiful intense green, and the best way to achieve this is to use Iranian pistachios. If you can't source these then you could add a drop or two of green food colouring, which is an authentic way to ensure the colour is correct, and is often added when cheaper pistachios are used.

This recipe requires some planning and time will need to be set aside for prep, though you could always split the work over two days. My advice would be to read through the recipe two or three times before getting stuck in.

Serves 10–12

unsalted butter, for greasing
flour, for dusting
6 free-range eggs
grated zest of ½ orange
280g caster sugar
130g plain flour, plus 2 tablespoons
¼ teaspoon fine salt
85g green pistachios (ideally Iranian)
360g icing sugar, plus extra to dust
1 free-range egg white, lightly beaten
1 or 2 drops green food
    colouring (optional)

2 tablespoons Grand Marnier
500g ricotta, drained overnight in
    a muslin-lined sieve, or 400g ricotta
    impastata (already drained of
    excess moisture)
1 teaspoon vanilla extract
½ teaspoon ground cinnamon
juice of 1 lemon
150g whole candied fruits (such
    as oranges, apricots and cherries),
    halved, plus candied citron, cut
    into strips

Preheat the oven to 180°C/160°C fan/Gas Mark 4. Butter and flour a 23cm round cake tin. Line the bottom and sides of a 30cm round, deep pie dish (or similar) with clingfilm.

Put the eggs, orange zest and 130g of the caster sugar into the bowl of a free-standing electric mixer and beat on high speed until pale and light. Fold in the 130g of flour and the salt. Pour the mixture into the cake tin and smooth the top. Bake for about 30 minutes or until the cake is golden and cooked through – a skewer inserted into the centre should come out clean. Set the tin on a wire rack to cool, then turn out the cake on to the rack. When cold, cut the cake across into 1cm strips.

Put the pistachios in a food processor with 120g of the icing sugar and blitz until finely ground. Add the egg white and the food colouring (if using) and pulse to form a smooth

...continued on page 246

paste, like marzipan. Dust a work surface with plenty of icing sugar and a little extra flour. Turn out the pistachio paste on to this and knead for 3 minutes. Roll out to 5mm thick, then cut into strips about 5cm wide and use to line the side of the pie dish with an overlap. Press any joins together so the pistachio paste makes a nice smooth and continuous ring.

Heat 75g of the remaining caster sugar with 75ml of water to dissolve. Remove from the heat and stir in the Grand Marnier.

In a large bowl whisk together the ricotta, vanilla extract, cinnamon and remaining 75g of caster sugar until smooth and creamy.

To assemble, line the bottom of the prepared pie dish with cake strips, cutting them to fit (you'll use about half). Sprinkle about half of the Grand Marnier syrup over the cake to moisten. Spoon the ricotta mixture on top of the cake and spread out to fill the pie dish, smoothing the top evenly. Cover the top of the ricotta mixture with the remaining cake strips, cutting to fit. Drizzle over the remaining syrup. Trim excess pistachio paste. Wrap the pie dish with clingfilm and chill.

Meanwhile, mix together the remaining 240g icing sugar and the lemon juice in a medium bowl to make a thick icing.

Invert the pie dish on to a serving dish or wooden board to unmould the cassata. Peel off the clingfilm. Pour the icing over the cassata to cover evenly. Decorate as you wish with the candied fruits and citron (you can get quite creative here). Place the cake in the fridge and leave for at least 2 hours, or overnight, to set.

Zeppole (Doughnuts)
with Almonds and Sultanas

Zeppole are eaten around many parts of Italy and rolled out as a celebration cake on the annual St Joseph's saint day – in fact another name for these is St Joseph's day fritters.

The Arabic origins of this doughnut and many other variants began with fried pastry dough, drizzled with honey as a simple, filling and sweet treat. The addition of spices and aromats such as cinnamon or ground cloves might be added for flavour.

Zeppole are far more refined and lighter than a simple fried pastry and the Italians have cleverly incorporated ricotta into this recipe which adds a fresh edge and also helps with the consistency, making it light.

They are incredibly versatile and you can top them with anything you like – candied fruits and poached citrus segments are a favourite, and I also like to dip them in melted milk chocolate. This version is thoroughly Sicilian, with the classic combination of almonds and sultanas whipped into a lightly spiced cream, which should be spooned onto the doughnuts as soon as they come out of the oil – the cream will melt down the sides and get very messy but that's the point!

Serves 4

2 litres vegetable oil, for deep-frying
125g plain flour, sifted
a pinch of salt
1½ teaspoons caster sugar
2 teaspoons baking powder
2 free-range eggs, beaten
245g ricotta
¼ teaspoon vanilla extract
grated zest of ½ orange
60g icing sugar, for dusting

Cream
150ml double cream
20g sultanas, roughly chopped
10g ground almonds
a pinch of ground cinnamon
10g icing sugar

First make the cream. Pour the double cream into a bowl and whip until doubled in volume and firm peaks have formed. Stir in the rest of the ingredients. Cover and keep in the fridge.

Pour the oil into a deep pan or deep-fat fryer and heat to 180°C.

While the oil is heating, put the flour, salt, caster sugar and baking powder into a saucepan and stir in the eggs, ricotta, vanilla extract and orange zest. Mix gently over a low heat to form a sticky batter.

Using a tablespoon, carefully drop dollops of the batter into the hot oil, cooking just a few at a time, and fry for 4 minutes or until golden brown – the doughnuts will turn over by themselves. Remove the doughnuts with a slotted spoon and drain on kitchen paper, then dust with the icing sugar. Serve with the cream spooned on top.

Cannoli
with Saffron Ricotta and Candied Fruits

Cannoli are a national dish of Sicily – you'll see them lined up in pastry shops, golden, deep-fried folded pastry tubes stuffed with cream or chocolate. I adore them and can put away three or four with a coffee in one sitting.

They originate from the Palermo and Messina regions where the Moors brought along similar fried desserts and introduced them to the locals, such as zainabs fingers (fried and stuffed with nuts) and quwanawt (fried dough tubes filled with dried fruits and nut pastes).

As the cannoli are deep fried you'll need a special cannoli tube to get the authentic finish – these are widely available to buy online.

Makes about 28

Pastry shells
375g plain flour, plus extra for dusting
4 tablespoons caster sugar
1 teaspoon ground cinnamon
¼ teaspoon salt
45g unsalted butter
2 free-range egg whites
2 free-range eggs, beaten
1 tablespoon Marsala wine
2 tablespoons distilled malt vinegar
500ml vegetable oil, for deep-frying

40g icing sugar, to dust
4 tablespoons finely chopped green
   pistachios (preferably Iranian)

Filling
750g ricotta
½ teaspoon saffron threads, soaked in
   1 teaspoon warm milk
250g icing sugar
2 teaspoons vanilla extract
120g finely diced candied fruits

First make the pastry dough. Mix together the flour, sugar, cinnamon and salt in a medium-sized bowl. Add the butter and rub in until it is in pieces no larger than peas. Make a well in the centre and pour in one of the egg whites, the beaten eggs, Marsala, vinegar and 2 tablespoons of cold water. Mix with a fork until the mixture becomes stiff, then finish mixing by hand, kneading on a clean surface. Add a bit more water if needed to bind it all together to make a dough, or add a bit more flour if the dough is too wet. Knead for about 10 minutes or until soft and smooth. Cover and chill for 1 hour.

Divide the dough into thirds and flatten each piece just enough to get it through the rollers of a pasta machine. One piece at a time, roll the dough through successively thinner settings until you have reached the thinnest setting. (If you don't have a pasta machine, roll out the dough by hand with a floured rolling pin as thinly and evenly as possible; dust the dough lightly with flour, if necessary.)

You will need to shape and deep-fry the cannoli shells in batches, the number depending on how many cannoli moulds you have. Place the sheet of dough on a lightly floured surface. Using a large glass or bowl, cut out twenty-eight 10–12.5cm rounds. Dust them with a light coating of flour (this will help you later in removing the shells from the moulds). Roll a round of dough around a cannoli mould, sealing the join with a bit of the second egg white.

...continued on page 252

Heat the oil in a deep pan or deep-fat fryer to 180°C.

Fry the pastry shells (on the moulds) a few at a time for 2 minutes or until lightly golden and slightly puffy. Use tongs to turn them so they colour all over. Carefully remove using the tongs and place on a wire rack set over kitchen paper. Cool just long enough so that you can handle them, then carefully twist each mould to remove the pastry shell – using a tea towel may help you get a better grip. Wipe off the cooled moulds and use them to shape and deep-fry more shells.

Once the pastry shells are completely cooled, they can be stored in an airtight container for up to 2 months. They are best if filled just before serving, or up to 1 hour ahead, as they can get soggy.

To make the filling, stir together the ricotta, saffron milk, icing sugar and vanilla extract, and fold in the candied fruits. Use a piping bag to pipe the filling into the shells, piping from the centre to one end, then doing the same from the other end. Dust with icing sugar, sprinkle with the pistachios and serve.

Crocetta of Caltanissetta

Caltanissetta is a commune in central Sicily occupied by the Arabs in 829 AD. The Arabs named the commune Qal'at al-Nisā which translates as 'fort of the women'. Over the years the name has become Italianised into its current form. The commune is famous for two things – its active and volatile volcanoes and this sweet fried pastry.

The crocetta has been recently rediscovered, after it took a hiatus in 1908 for a century, by a local pastry chef and four Benedictine sisters from the commune. The crocetta itself could not be more influenced by the Moors love of sweets, nuts and fruits: laden with almonds, pistachios, cinnamon, lemon purée and orange and then deep fried.

I find it fascinating that the cake, in all its Arabic glory, has become a symbol of the Benedictine-Catholic church and is prepared for the Holy Crucifix festivities in Caltanissetta. How seamlessly the two cultures intertwined, each retaining an identity while creating something unique together.

The original recipe is a closely guarded secret – this is my version.

Makes about 30

Pastry
150g plain flour, sifted, plus extra
    for dusting
½ teaspoon baking powder
50g ground almonds
1½ tablespoons icing sugar
1½ teaspoons ground cinnamon
grated zest of ½ unwaxed lemon
2 free-range egg yolks
50ml extra virgin olive oil
1 free-range egg, beaten, for sealing
    the crocette
olive oil
50ml runny honey

a handful of green pistachios
    (preferably Iranian), very
    finely chopped

Filling
90g unsalted butter, at room
    temperature
100g caster sugar
grated zest of 2 unwaxed lemons
100ml lemon juice
2 free-range eggs, beaten
1 tablespoon finely chopped candied
    lemon peel

In a bowl, mix together the flour, baking powder, ground almonds, icing sugar, cinnamon and zest. In a separate bowl, whisk together the egg yolks and olive oil, then mix into the flour a little at a time to form a dough. Knead the dough with your hands, adding a splash or two of cold water, until smooth and quite firm. Wrap and chill for an hour.

Roll out the dough on a floured surface to about 5mm thickness. Cut the pastry into discs about 5cm in diameter using a round cutter. Arrange the discs on a floured tray.

To make the filling, put the butter, sugar and lemon zest and juice in a saucepan and cook over a low heat for 2–3 minutes or until melted and smooth. Strain the eggs through a sieve into the mix, whisking all the time – this will prevent the eggs from scrambling. Continue

...continued on page 254

to cook gently, stirring constantly, until the curd thickens, then immediately remove from the heat and pour into a bowl to cool. Stir in the chopped candied peel. Keep in the fridge until ready to use.

Put about ½ teaspoon of the lemon filling in the centre of each disc of dough, leaving a good edge clear – you want to be able to fold it over to create a half-moon shape. Brush half the edge of each disc with beaten egg, then fold over and press to seal – try to avoid trapping any air. Use your finger or a fork to crimp the seal. Place the tray of crocette in the fridge to chill for 20 minutes.

Heat a 2cm depth of olive oil in a large sauté pan to about 160°C. Fry the crocette in 2 or 3 batches for 2 minutes on each side or until the pastry is crisp and golden brown. When cooked transfer to kitchen paper to drain.

Drizzle the honey over the crocette, then sprinkle with the chopped pistachios. Leave to cool before serving.

Lemon and Anise Biscuits

These Ibiza-style little shortbread biscuits are packed full of fragrant lemon and a hint of anise. I like to have them with coffee or you can crumble them up and sprinkle over ice cream or granita.

Makes about 20

Candied lemon
200g caster sugar
2 large unwaxed, knobbly lemons, cut into 5mm rounds with a sharp knife (pips removed)

Biscuits
200g plain flour, plus extra for dusting

70g caster sugar, plus extra for sprinkling
135g unsalted butter, diced and chilled
juice of ½ lemon
grated zest of 1 unwaxed lemon
½ teaspoon ground star anise

First make the candied lemon. Line a tray with baking parchment. Put the sugar in a large sauté pan with 200ml of water and bring to the boil over a medium heat. Simmer to dissolve the sugar. Make a layer of lemon slices in the syrup and cook for 10 minutes to soften and become candied. Transfer to the tray. Repeat to candy the remaining lemon slices. Set aside to cool and set.

To make the biscuit dough, mix together the flour and sugar in a bowl, then rub in the butter with your fingertips to form fine crumbs. Add the lemon juice, zest and anise and mix to form a dough. Cover in clingfilm and chill for 1 hour.

Preheat the oven to 180°C/160°C fan/Gas Mark 4.

Roll out the dough on a floured surface to about 5mm thick and cut out 8cm discs with a round cutter. Transfer the discs to lightly floured baking trays and bake for 20 minutes or until the biscuits are a light golden brown. Cool on a wire rack.

Place a candied lemon slice on top of each biscuit before serving.

Top left: Crocetta of Caltanissetta (see page 253)
Bottom left: Lemon and Anise Biscuits (see page 255)
Right: Balearic-style Flaó Baked Honey, Mint and Orange Cheesecake with Pine Nuts (see page 258)

Balearic-style Flaó
Baked Honey, Mint and Orange Cheesecake with Pine Nuts

This is a light, fresh, baked cheesecake inspired by the Ibizan flaó, an unusual goat's cheesecake that has its roots set firmly in the Balearic's Moorish heritage. Traditionally the cheesecake is packed with anise seeds, liqueur and fresh mint and has a moist pastry crust housing the baked cheese mix. I love the addition of soft goat's cheese – it has a lovely grassy, floral flavour that naturally lightens the cake.

My version includes chopped pine nuts for texture and orange and orange blossom honey instead of the anise.

You should serve the cake when still warm with some sweetened yoghurt or cream served on the side.

Serves 8

400g cream cheese, at
    room temperature
200g soft goat's cheese, at
    room temperature
50g caster sugar
4 large free-range eggs
125ml orange blossom or other runny
    honey, plus extra for drizzling
3 drops of orange flower water
2 teaspoons cornflour
½ handful of mint, leaves picked
½ teaspoon lemon juice
grated zest of 1 large orange
20g pine nuts, lightly toasted

Pastry
30g unsalted butter, at room
    temperature
30g caster sugar
1 large free-range egg, beaten
1 tablespoon olive oil
grated zest of ½ orange
200g plain flour, sifted, plus extra
    for dusting
a pinch of salt

First make the pastry. Whisk the butter with the sugar in a free-standing electric mixer, or using a hand-held electric mixer, until light and combined. With the mixer running, add the egg, olive oil and orange zest and mix for 2 minutes to ensure everything is well combined.

Mix the flour with the salt, then fold into the egg mix to form a pastry dough. Knead (by hand) for a minute or so. Shape into a ball, wrap in clingfilm and place in the fridge to rest for 15 minutes.

Preheat the oven to 160°C/140°C fan/Gas Mark 3. Grease a 20cm round pie dish or tin.

Lay out a large piece of baking parchment and dust it with flour. Roll out the pastry dough on the floured parchment into a round about 5mm thick. Roll up on to the pin, then roll back out over the dish. Press the pastry into the dish to line the bottom and sides, ensuring there are no air pockets. Leave a good overhang of pastry around the edge. Prick the bottom lightly with a fork, then line the pastry case with baking parchment and fill with baking beans. Set the dish on a baking tray. Bake for 20 minutes or until the pastry is a light golden brown. Remove from the oven to cool.

While the pastry case is baking, make the cheese filling. Use an electric mixer to beat together the cheeses and caster sugar until smooth and creamy. Add the eggs, honey, flower water and cornflour and mix until everything is fully incorporated. Finally, stir in half the mint leaves, the lemon juice and orange zest. Pour the mix into the pastry case, filling it as much as you dare.

Return the flaó to the oven and bake for 30 minutes or until the filling is just set with a slight wobble and the pastry is golden brown.

Remove from the oven. Sprinkle with the remaining mint leaves and the pine nuts and drizzle over some extra honey. Leave to cool completely, then trim the pastry edge. Serve in the dish at the table for all to share.

Pistachio, Orange and Cardamom Tart
with Gran Torres and Goat's Milk Yoghurt

I like to use the super green Iranian pistachios for this recipe, not only for their vibrant colour but also for their fresh, sweet flavour. The cardamom works beautifully alongside the fresh orange flavour.

Gran Torres is a delicious orange brandy liqueur from Spain that I love to add in desserts for a little kick. If you can't find it then another dry orange liqueur will do.

Serves 8–10

220g plain flour, sifted, plus extra for dusting
a pinch of salt
10 cardamom pods, seeds removed and ground in a pestle and mortar
140g unsalted butter, diced
1 free-range egg yolk
goat's milk yoghurt, to serve

Filling
280g green pistachios (ideally Iranian)
180g blanched almonds

240g caster sugar
¼ teaspoon freshly ground cardamom seeds (from pod)
125ml fresh orange juice
5 free-range egg yolks
grated zest of 1 orange
20ml Gran Torres Orange Liqueur or Grand Marnier

First make the pastry. Put the flour, salt and ground cardamom seeds in a food processor and blitz to mix. With the machine running, gradually add the butter, piece by piece, and pulse for a few minutes until reduced to tiny lumps. Mix in the egg yolk. Tip the mix into a bowl and knead together for a few minutes to make a dough. Wrap in clingfilm and leave to rest in the fridge for an hour or so.

Roll out the dough on a floured surface and use to line a 24cm round, loose-bottomed tart tin. Prick the pastry with a fork before placing in the freezer to chill for an hour or so.

Preheat the oven to 180°C/160°C fan/Gas Mark 4. Line the tart case with baking parchment and fill with baking beans. Bake blind for 20–25 minutes or until the pastry is cooked and has turned a light golden brown. Remove the paper and beans, then set aside to cool. Leave the oven on.

For the filling, blitz the nuts, sugar and cardamom in a food processor until fine and smooth. With the machine running, slowly add the orange juice to form a smooth paste. Add 4 of the egg yolks and the orange zest and blitz for a further couple of minutes. Add the liqueur.

Spread the filling in the tart case. Bake for 15 minutes or until the top has just set. Lightly beat the remaining egg yolk and brush over the surface. Bake for a further 10 minutes or until glazed. Leave to cool for at least an hour before serving. Top each piece of tart with a dollop of rich, creamy and floral goat's milk yoghurt.

DRINKS

While the Moors did not drink alcohol they harnessed their technological aptitude and scholarly pursuit of science to develop the first still, the essential device needed to distil alcohol. These stills, or alembic in Arabic, found their way onto the Iberian peninsula where the non-Muslims discovered that distilling grape must (the seeds, stems and skins left over from wine production) produced a very potent neutral flavoured spirit, very similar to the Italian grappa.

The wonderful drinks that follow combine Moorish flavours with produce familiar to the Iberian peninsula, southern Italy and Sicily.

I wanted to include a lovely limoncello but absolutely not one like the mass-produced, sickly shots at the end of a mediocre Italian meal that so many of us will have suffered. The fresh and vibrant artisanal liqueur you can find in southern Italy and Sicily and which I've created here is a completely different delight altogether (see page 274). I've also included a fantastically refreshing Bergamot-ade (see page 269), a twist on lemonade using delicious and fragrant bergamots that are in season over the winter months and grown mainly in Sicily and Calabria – another gift from the Moors.

You could finish off with my Cinnamon-spiced Hot Chocolate (see page 278) and a good glug of Spanish brandy if you like – perfect bedfellows especially when you introduce a cinnamon cream into the mix. And if you need a little pep up, an affogato always does the trick – my spin includes an exotic hit of cardamom in the form of an ice cream and then a shot of dark, rich and complex Pedro Ximenez sherry (see page 276).

Apple and Cumin Martini

Through trial and error I've found that apple and cumin work very well together – the sweet and sour of the apple contrasting with the warm, aromatic spice. There are so many quality gins around now but some can be very heavy on the botanicals which are great in a simple G&T but for this, with so many flavours at play, a more neutral flavoured gin is best. My favourite is Tanqueray No. 10.

Serves 4-ish

1 apple, peeled, cored and cut into small pieces
2 tablespoons light brown sugar
½ teaspoon cumin seeds, roughly ground with a pestle and mortar
1 teaspoon cider vinegar (preferably organic)

40ml Italian vermouth
250ml quality gin

Garnish
thin apple slices
cumin seeds

Put the apple and sugar into a small pan and cook over a low heat until starting to caramelise. Add the crushed cumin and cook for 3 minutes before stirring in the vinegar. Reduce to a glaze. Add 150ml of water and cook for 5 minutes or until reduced by half. Pour into a small food processor and blitz until smoothly puréed. Pass the purée through a sieve. Leave to cool, then chill for at least a couple of hours.

Chill 4 martini glasses.

Fill a large cocktail shaker with ice. Pour over the vermouth, followed by the gin and then add the purée. Shake vigorously 14 to 16 times, then strain through a sieve into the chilled glasses. Garnish each glass with a thin slice of apple and a little sprinkle of cumin seeds.

Spiced Gin with Blood Orange

I choose a fairly neutral gin for this such as Tanqueray – too many botanical flavours will interfere with the spice hit.

You could make this with other bittersweet oranges out of season and it will still work a treat, albeit without the reddy-pink tinge of the bloods.

The recipe below is for making on the day of drinking, though you could make the spiced gin ahead of time in a larger batch and then leave it to develop and improve with time.

Serves 6

Spiced gin
2 cinnamon sticks, roughly crushed
1 teaspoon coriander seeds,
    lightly crushed
6 cloves, broken up
pared zest of 2 blood oranges
50ml runny honey
400ml quality gin

To finish
400ml blood orange juice (from
    4–5 oranges)
1 blood orange, peeled and segmented
6 thin slices of blood orange,
    to garnish
coriander seeds, to garnish

For the spiced gin, put the spices and orange zest into a saucepan and cook over a medium heat until the seeds pop and the zest starts to release its oils. This will take 6–7 minutes. Remove from the heat and stir in the honey.

Transfer the spice mix to a container and pour in the gin. Mix well, crushing the spices with a fork as you go. Cover and leave in the fridge for at least 2 hours or until ready to make the cocktail.

Chill 6 glasses.

Half fill a cocktail shaker with ice. Strain in the spiced gin followed by the orange juice. Add the orange segments. Using a long-handled cocktail spoon, stir about 20 times, then strain into the chilled glasses. Garnish each with a slice of orange and a sprinkle of coriander seeds.

Iced Averna, Watermelon and Fresh Mint

Amaro Averna is a traditional Sicilian liqueur flavoured with spices, citrus, roots and herbs and then finished with caramel to give the drink its distinct colouring.

Averna is usually drunk at the end of a meal, either neat or with a little ice added as a digestif, though I like to turn it into a longer, more refreshing drink with the addition of mint, cooling watermelon and a splash of tonic.

Serves 2

100g watermelon flesh (pith and
  seeds removed)
a good handful of mint leaves
tonic water, to top up the glasses
100ml Averna

Place 2 highball glasses in the freezer.

Put the watermelon in a blender along with two-thirds of the mint leaves and a little tonic water. Blitz to a purée.

Fill a cocktail shaker half full with ice. Pour in the Averna and then the watermelon purée. Shake vigorously for 2 minutes, then strain the liquid into the chilled glasses. Add a couple of ice cubes to each glass and top up with tonic. Garnish with the remaining mint leaves and serve.

Bergamot-ade

Bergamot, the highly perfumed and tart citrus fruit from Calabria in south-west Italy, becomes the ultimate thirst quencher when turned into an alternative to lemonade.

The bergamot fruits are only available in the winter months but you can buy the fresh juice year round.

Serves 6–8

5 bergamots, plus extra wedges
   for serving
200g golden caster sugar
400ml boiling water

Cut the bergamots in half and squeeze out all the juice with a lemon squeezer. Transfer it to a big jug and add the sugar. Carefully pour in the boiling water. Using a long-handled wooden spoon, stir until all of the sugar has dissolved.

Add 600ml of cold water and stir everything together. Taste the drink and add a little more sugar, if desired. Pour into bottles, put the lids on and leave in the fridge overnight. The bergamot-ade is now ready to drink.

Pour the bergamot-ade into tumblers, add bergamot wedges and ice cubes, and serve.

Rose and Rhubarb Fizz

Rhubarb isn't usually associated with Moorish cuisine, however the North Africans have been using it for centuries as a sharp accompaniment to fatty meats or blended to a purée and served very cold as a refreshing thirst quencher.

The rhubarb will make more syrup than you need but it will keep in the fridge for a few weeks and is delicious over ice cream.

Serves 2

120ml gin (such as Hendricks or Tanqueray), kept in the freezer
10ml dry vermouth (such as Dolin de Chambery)
10ml lemon juice
20ml lime juice
8–10 drops of rose water

1 large free-range egg white
rosé champagne, to top up the glasses
rose petals, to garnish

Rhubarb syrup
200g rhubarb
200g caster sugar

Preheat the oven to 200°C/180°C fan/Gas Mark 6 and chill 2 champagne glasses.

For the syrup, put the rhubarb and sugar into a small baking tray or dish with 250ml of water. Cook in the oven for 30 minutes, then strain the rhubarb syrup into a jug and cool.

Put the gin, vermouth, lemon and lime juices, rose water, egg white and 70ml of the rhubarb syrup into a cocktail shaker (without ice). Shake hard (this is called dry shaking). Open the shaker, fill with ice and shake again, very hard, for as long as you can but at least a few minutes.

Strain into the chilled glasses and top with the champagne. Carefully garnish with a few rose petals, then serve.

Home-made Limoncello

Limoncello is one of the most popular drinks in the south of Italy, served chilled at the end of a meal or as a little refresher on a blazing hot afternoon.

Though simple to make, there are two cardinal rules to observe. Firstly the lemons should be in season, unwaxed, knobbly and preferably from the Amalfi coast (traditional recipes use only lemons from Sorrento) – the lemons should be full of flavour and headily perfumed. Secondly you will need to get hold of some 100 per cent proof alcohol, such as a vodka (Smirnoff has one) or a grappa.

With these two rules followed you'll be able to make the most delicious, refreshing and natural drink, a world away from the ultra sweet and sickly commercial types you get offered in the more dubious trattorias and restaurants.

Makes 1 litre

6 large, unwaxed Amalfi lemons
750ml 100 per cent proof alcohol
250g caster sugar

Pare the zest from the lemons, ensuring there's no pith, and place in a jar or other container with the alcohol. Close the jar or container and leave to infuse in a cool spot for 10 days.

Put the sugar into a saucepan with 225ml of water and bring to the boil, stirring to dissolve the sugar. Simmer for a minute to create a syrup. Remove from the heat and leave to cool completely.

Strain the lemon-infused alcohol through a fine sieve lined with a clean tea towel or muslin (so you get a really fine strain) into a large jug. Stir in the cooled sugar syrup. Pour the limoncello into 1–2 bottles and seal them. Leave to mature in a dark, cool spot for 10 days.

Now store the bottles in the freezer – the alcohol content will stop the limoncello from freezing solid – and serve in cold glasses.

Cardamom Affogato with PX Shot

This cardamom ice cream is sublime – the cardamom's heady scent and aromatic, resinous flavour is intoxicating. It will make more than you need but will happily keep in the freezer for a month or so.

I often serve it with yoghurt and grated bitter chocolate or drizzled with date molasses, but perhaps my favourite variation is as an affogato, with rich, slightly bitter coffee poured over followed by a little shot of the sweet sherry Pedro Ximinez, famed for its dried fruit and spice flavours.

Serves 4

4 shots of hot, freshly brewed, medium-strong black coffee
4 x 25ml shots Pedro Ximenez sherry

Cardamom ice cream
300ml full-cream milk
200ml double cream

7 green cardamom pods, crushed
4 free-range egg yolks
100g caster sugar

First make the ice cream. Heat the milk and cream with the cardamom pods until almost boiling. Remove from the heat and leave to cool and infuse for an hour, then strain through a sieve into a clean pan. Place on the heat and warm through again.

Whisk together the egg yolks and sugar until smooth but not particularly aerated. Carefully ladle some of the warm cream mixture on to the yolk mix and whisk, then add more cream and whisk again. Pour the egg mixture into the pan with the rest of the warm cream. Return the pan to a gentle heat and stir until the custard thickens – don't let it get much over 60°C or it will go all lumpy. Allow to cool, then churn to freeze.

About 10 minutes before serving, remove the ice cream from the freezer. Scoop a ball of ice cream into each small heatproof glass or cup. Pour a shot of coffee over each scoop and then a shot of PX. Serve immediately.

Cinnamon-spiced Hot Chocolate
with Spanish Brandy

This is a really indulgent hot chocolate made all the more delicious with the addition of cinnamon and a good pinch of salt.

I've used Spanish brandy but a dark rum or whisky will work well.

Serves 6

900ml full-cream milk
140g dark chocolate (with 70% cocoa solids), grated
60g milk chocolate, grated
200ml double cream, plus 100ml extra for whipping (optional)

2 pinches of sea salt
½ teaspoon ground cinnamon
180ml Spanish brandy or other quality brandy

Warm about 400ml of the milk in a saucepan over a medium heat. Add the dark and milk chocolate and stir until melted. Stir in the remaining milk and the 200ml of cream. Bring back to a simmer but do not boil. Stir in the salt and cinnamon.

Divide the brandy among 6 hot chocolate glasses or mugs (300ml each). Pour in the hot chocolate and stir a couple of times to mix the brandy through, then serve. For extra indulgence, whip the 100ml of cream to soft peaks and top the hot chocolate with this (serve with a spoon).

SAUCES & MARINADES

Ajo Blanco

Ajo blanco is the original cold soup of southern Spain, as popular now as when it was introduced by the Moors during the occupation.

You could say it was the original instasoup – dried nuts and bread, ground in a pestle and mortar and then hydrated with water and vinegar when needed.

Delicious on a hot summer's day served very cold with a sprinkling of fresh black grapes and some freshly chopped herbs, or as a dressing for grilled meats and albondigas.

Vinegar and almonds are the predominant flavours in the soup so try to source the best quality you can find.

Makes about 800ml

50g crustless day-old white bread, ripped into small pieces
250g blanched almonds
450–550ml ice-cold water
2 garlic cloves, very finely chopped

1½ tablespoons moscatel vinegar or white balsamic
1 tablespoon extra virgin olive oil
sea salt and black pepper

Put the bread into a bowl and pour over a little cold water. Leave to soak for about 15 minutes.

Put the almonds into a food processor and blitz to a fine powder – the almonds will stick to the side of the processor bowl. Pour in 200ml of the cold water and continue to blitz until you have a loose paste. Add the garlic and blitz for a further 2 minutes.

Drain the bread and add it to the almond paste in the food processor along with the vinegar and olive oil. Continue to blitz, slowly adding the remaining water.

Season the ajo blanco, then transfer to the fridge to chill for at least 1 hour before serving.

Alioli

Alioli in its most rustic form is a simple emulsion of pounded raw garlic and olive oil, a fiery concoction used for multiple purposes – dips for vegetables, poured over grilled fish and meats or whisked into soups.

I prefer the lighter, more refined version similar to a garlic mayonnaise. It's the essence of the Mediterranean and you can use it with pretty much everything.

It's also a great vessel for other flavours.

Makes about 200ml

1 large free-range egg yolk
½ teaspoon Dijon mustard
½ garlic clove, very finely chopped
100ml vegetable oil

100ml extra virgin olive oil
lemon juice, to taste
white wine vinegar, to taste
sea salt and black pepper

Place the egg yolk in a mixing bowl with the mustard and garlic. Begin whisking and start slowly adding the vegetable oil to emulsify. After some of the oil has been incorporated into the yolk, you can speed up the rate at which you are adding the vegetable oil and then the olive oil. When all the oils have been added, season with salt and pepper and add lemon juice and vinegar to taste.

Saffron alioli
Soak 1 teaspoon saffron threads in 2 teaspoons hot water until cooled. Make the alioli as above, then whisk in the saffron water. Leave to infuse in the fridge for an hour before whisking again to spread the colour and flavour through the alioli.

Almond alioli
Finely chop the leaves picked from a sprig of rosemary. Put into a mortar and add 1 tablespoon of very finely chopped blanched almonds and 20ml of extra virgin olive oil. Pound with the pestle until you have a coarse green paste. Make the alioli as above, replacing 50ml of the olive oil with the almond-rosemary paste. Leave to infuse in the fridge for an hour before serving.

Orange alioli
Put the juice of 2 oranges in a small pan and boil to reduce to a glaze. Set aside to cool. Make the alioli as above, then whisk in the orange glaze.

Harissa

Harissa in North Africa is the equivalent of tomato ketchup in the UK, Europe and the Americas. More a condiment than a sauce and something that's used on everything – eggs, meat, vegetables, you name it. Harissa is a far more complex and versatile sauce than ketchup, with many hundreds of variations found over North Africa, each one using a unique mix of peppers, spices and, on occasions, essential oils.

Harissa is all about the peppers and if the Spanish hadn't introduced them into North Africa in the 15th century then it might never have been created. You are as likely to find harissa in Andalucía as you are in Morocco.

I cook the chillies over a barbecue to get a really authentic smokiness into the harissa – it makes all the difference.

Makes about 250ml

14 fresh, red finger-length chillies
1½ teaspoons coriander seeds
½ teaspoon cumin seeds
½ teaspoon caraway seeds
5 garlic cloves, roughly chopped

1 teaspoon sea salt flakes
2 teaspoons tomato purée
2½ teaspoons lemon juice
2 tablespoons light extra virgin olive oil

Prepare and light a charcoal fire in a barbecue for medium heat. Cook the chillies on the barbecue for about 20 minutes, turning them to blacken the skins all over, until the flesh is tender. Transfer to a plastic bag, or a bowl covered with clingfilm, to steam and cool.

Remove the stalk and peel the chillies. Split them lengthways and scrape out the seeds with a knife; discard the seeds. Don't rinse the chillies – you'll lose the smoky flavour. Set aside.

Toast the coriander, cumin and caraway seeds in a dry frying pan until fragrant, making sure they don't burn. Pummel to a fine powder with a pestle and mortar or in a spice grinder. Add the chillies, garlic and salt, and grind to a fine paste. Stir in the remaining ingredients. Set aside for at least 1 hour before using, to allow the flavours to develop.

Clockwise from left: Salsa Moresca (see page 289); Alioli (see page 282); Harissa (see page 283); Pistachio Dukkah (see page 287); Salmoriglio (see page 288); Mojo Verde (see page 286); Romesco Sauce (see page 288).

Mojo Picón

A classic Canary island sauce traditionally made using Palermo peppers grown on the island of Palma, the spiritual home of the sauce. The peppers are dried out in the sun then slowly rehydrated, ground and mixed with garlic, bread, vinegar and olive oil. It's a sunshine sauce and one of my favourites to be spooned over pretty much anything in need of a flavour lift – the Canary Islanders love tossing freshly cooked potatoes with it. I also like to stir it into stews and braises at the end of cooking to add depth, heat and to thicken.

If you can find the Palermo peppers then great, otherwise dried Ñora peppers will work or any other quality Spanish deli peppers.

Makes about 250ml

4 dried smoky-sweet red peppers (such as Palermo or Ñora)
2 teaspoons dried chilli flakes
¼ teaspoon ground cumin
4 garlic cloves

1–2 slices stale white bread (crusts trimmed if very dry)
150ml extra virgin olive oil
½ teaspoon sea salt
25ml sherry vinegar, or to taste

Soak the peppers in warm water for 30 minutes to rehydrate. When they are ready, drain well and remove the seeds and stalks. Put the peppers into a blender along with the chilli flakes, cumin, peeled garlic and bread. With the machine running, slowly drizzle in the oil and then 50ml of water to create a paste. Add the salt and vinegar. Taste to check the seasoning. The paste will initially be very strong and fiery but the flavours will mellow over a day or so.

Mojo Verde

The wonderfully fresh mojo verde is a punchy dressing originating from the Canary Islands, ideal for spooning over grilled meats and fish. I often serve it as a dip for crunchy raw vegetables.

Makes about 200ml

½ green pepper
1 fresh green chilli, deseeded
½ teaspoon ground cumin
100g coriander with stalks
50g flat-leaf parsley

20ml red wine vinegar
100ml extra virgin olive oil
10g herb fennel
sea salt and black pepper

Put everything in a blender or food processor and blitz to a coarse paste. Season to taste.

Pine Nut, Cumin and Milk Sauce

This is a nut-thickened sauce beloved of the Moors. Pine nuts (not strictly nuts but seeds) have a unique sweet flavour that translates beautifully into a sauce. I serve this slightly looser as a cold 'sauce' and if thicker as a condiment for spreading – it's just a case of altering the milk quantity.

If you decide to toast the nuts you will get a deep, nutty, toasty flavour, while if left untoasted the nuts will be cleaner and fresher.

It can also be served warm and is delicious with chicken and pork dishes.

Makes about 250ml

100g pine nuts
½ teaspoon ground cumin
150–200ml full-cream cow's or goat's milk
1 tablespoon extra virgin olive oil
sea salt and black pepper

If you like, toast the pine nuts lightly in a dry pan. Put the nuts in a saucepan with the cumin and milk (150ml if you want a thick sauce; 200ml if you want a thinner sauce). Slowly bring to the boil, then simmer for 3 minutes. Remove from the heat and cool for 10 minutes before transferring to a food processor. Blitz to a very smooth purée. Season well, then add the olive oil and blitz again to combine.

You can also alter the consistency at this stage with more milk, if required.

Pistachio Dukkah

Dukkah has its origins in Egypt. The concept of using nuts and spices as both a flavouring and a thickener is now widespread throughout North Africa and the Mediterranean. I leave my dukkah quite coarse as I like to retain texture and tend to use it more like a dressing to be spooned over roasted vegetables or soft cheese.

Hazelnuts are the classic tried and tested base but I've used pistachios here, which after a while turn a stunning green and taste delicious.

Makes about 20ml

50g sesame seeds
10g nigella seeds
5g cumin seeds, lightly toasted in a dry pan
25g coriander seeds

about 150ml extra virgin olive oil
juice of ½ lemon
50g green pistachios (ideally Iranian)
sea salt and black pepper

Put the sesame seeds and all the spice seeds in a mortar and crush with the pestle for a few minutes to break up. Transfer to a bowl and add the oil and lemon juice.

Chop the pistachios into small pieces and add to the bowl. Season to taste. Leave at room temperature for an hour or so to allow the flavours to develop before using.

Romesco Sauce

I have been making romesco sauce from various recipes for many, many years. The authentic, original technique is a time-consuming process involving gently roasting peppers and tomatoes and peeling their blistered skins, then putting the flesh in a mixer or pestle and mortar to blend. However, this quick and easy recipe is as good as any I've made before. The trick is to source peeled piquillo peppers – they can be found in Spanish and European delis in tins. The peppers have been wood roasted and then hand-peeled, which gives the romesco its unique flavour. This will keep in the fridge for up to 10 days.

Makes about 250ml

30g blanched almonds, toasted
30g walnuts, toasted
1 garlic clove, crushed
200g roasted, peeled red peppers from
    a jar (such as piquillo) or roasted,
    peeled fresh red peppers, deseeded
¼ teaspoon hot smoked paprika

¼ teaspoon cayenne pepper
1 slice stale sourdough bread
1 teaspoon tomato purée
2 teaspoons sherry vinegar, or to taste
2 tablespoons extra virgin olive oil
sea salt and black pepper

Simply put everything in a blender or food processor, season and pulse-blitz to make a coarse purée.

Salmoriglio

Salmoriglio is a simple southern Italian preparation that has its roots in North African cuisine. Lemon and garlic are the dominant flavours here, typical of the punchy dressings found in the Middle East to accompany smoky grilled meats and fish and to marinade and preserve. The most well-known preparation is for Sicilian grilled sword fish steaks. The fish is marinated in the salmoriglio for an hour or so, grilled over wood and then finished with more of the dressing, perfectly showing off its versatility as both a marinade and a sauce.

If you can, try to source the exquisitely fragrant Amalfi lemons, otherwise an organic, knobbly variety will suffice. My version is finished with fresh marjoram leaves, though flat-leaf parsley, oregano or even mint would work well.

Makes about 250ml

200ml extra virgin olive oil
100ml fresh lemon juice (from
    2–3 lemons)
2 garlic cloves, crushed with some sea
    salt in a pestle and mortar

a handful of herbs (such as marjoram),
    leaves picked
sea salt and black pepper

Put the oil, lemon juice, garlic and 200ml of water in a bowl and whisk together. Season with salt and pepper, then leave for an hour to allow the flavours to develop. When ready to use, stir in the fresh herbs.

Salsa Moresca

This is an unusual Sicilian sauce with clear Moorish origins. The word *Moresca* is Italian for 'Moorish', as well as a name of a dance that was introduced by the Moors into Spain becoming popular over Europe in the 15th and 16th centuries.

It is primarily made and eaten in a specific area around Ragusa and Modica, both beautiful Baroque towns in the southern part of the island. Typically used as a pasta sauce but can be used for many things, I particularly enjoy it with grilled squids or tossed through with freshly steamed mussels.

The sauce features typically Moorish flavours of sweet and sour and can be made with either salted anchovies or bottarga (dried mullet roes) or even both.

Makes about 250ml

olive oil
1 slice day-old bread, turned into breadcrumbs
150g bottarga, grated, or salted anchovies, finely chopped (or a 50/50 mix of both)
2 garlic cloves, finely chopped
a small handful of flat-leaf parsley, finely chopped
½ teaspoon ground cinnamon

2 teaspoons caster sugar
grated zest and juice of 1 orange
grated zest and juice of ½ unwaxed lemon
150ml extra virgin olive oil
2 teaspoons red wine vinegar
1 fresh red chilli, finely chopped
50g pine nuts
sea salt and black pepper

Set a sauté pan over a low heat and add a glug of olive oil, then gently fry the breadcrumbs until lightly golden. Drain and reserve.

Put the bottarga and/or anchovies and the garlic in a mortar and pound with the pestle to a paste. Add the parsley, cinnamon, breadcrumbs and sugar and continue to pound. Pound in the citrus zests and juices and some seasoning followed by the oil and vinegar. Stir in the chilli and pine nuts.

If you don't have a pestle and mortar then a blender or small food processor will do the job. Just make sure you pulse-blitz – the result should be coarse and rustic.

Smoked Paprika, Cumin and Vinegar Marinade

This is my go-to for pork, lamb and beef, powerful meats with bold enough flavours to stand up to this no-holds-barred marinade. It involves flavour combinations that exemplifies the essence of Moorish cuisine – sweet, sour, spice and the heady earthiness of cumin.

Makes about 350ml

1 tablespoon cumin seeds
4 tablespoons sweet smoked paprika
2 tablespoons ground cumin
2 teaspoons coriander seeds, crushed
50ml red wine vinegar

2 garlic cloves, finely chopped
150ml extra virgin olive oil
juice of 1 lemon
sea salt and black pepper

Heat the cumin seeds in a small dry pan until they start to release their oil and become fragrant. Immediately tip into a mortar and crush lightly with the pestle.

Whisk together all the other ingredients, then add the crushed cumin seeds and season well. Leave the marinade for at least an hour to allow the flavours to develop before using. This quantity is good for 4 steaks or equivalent. Double the recipe for a lamb shoulder or a pork rack.

Tomato, Almond and Chilli Pesto

This is a delicious spin on a classic pesto that I stumbled across in Sicily. It goes brilliantly with everything from pasta to pizzas to grilled meats, fish and vegetables.

Buy a good quality jar of roasted tomatoes for this recipe, ideally one that indicates 'fire or wood-roasted' – they will have a deep, sweet-smoky flavour that will bring out the best in the pesto.

Makes about 250ml

50g blanched almonds
200g roasted tomatoes from
   a jar, drained
a handful of basil, leaves picked
1 tablespoon red wine vinegar

½ teaspoon dried chilli flakes
50ml extra virgin olive oil
40g Parmesan, freshly grated
sea salt and back pepper

Toast the almonds in a dry pan over a medium-high heat, stirring frequently, for 3–5 minutes or until golden and fragrant. Allow to cool slightly.

Transfer the almonds to a food processor and blitz until finely ground. Add the tomatoes, basil, vinegar and chilli flakes. With the machine running, drizzle in the oil in a steady stream until fully incorporated. Stir in the Parmesan and season well. The pesto will keep in an airtight jar in the fridge for at least 2 weeks.

Yoghurt, Garlic, Cumin and Chilli Marinade

A good yoghurt marinade has three important features; it adds a delicious acidic tang to whatever it's marinating, it naturally tenderises proteins due to its calcium content, and due to its thick consistency creates a crust when grilled or roasted.

I use this marinade for various meats or fish such as sardines, mackerel, sea bass and also large prawns. The addition of a little sumac in the yoghurt brings out the natural acidity.

Makes about 250ml

200ml thick plain yoghurt
2 teaspoons ground cumin
2 garlic cloves, finely chopped
a handful of mint leaves, chopped

1 teaspoon dried chilli flakes
½ teaspoon ground sumac
juice of ½ lemon
sea salt and black pepper

Whisk together all the ingredients with 50ml of water. Season. Leave in the fridge for an hour before using to allow the flavours to develop. This is enough marinade for 12 large prawns or 4 mackerel fillets.

INDEX

About the Author

Ben's love of food started at an early age in the seaside town of Skegness. Very busy parents meant that Ben spent a lot of time with his Jewish grandmother, a feeder if ever there was one and a brilliant home cook. Everything she made tasted delicious and the care and love she put into making things for her family was evident.

At 19-years-old he moved to London to become a professional chef as a 3rd commis chef (the lowest rank in the chef world) at The Ritz, London. A baptism of fire ensued over the next two years followed by a move to the ultra cool restaurant Coast, where Ben worked with Jason Atherton and Stephen Terry.

After working at a number of Michelin-starred restaurants Ben found himself at a high-end Italian restaurant in London's Mayfair which proved to be the turning point for his style. The kitchen's focus was on seasonality, with impeccable produce treated with the utmost respect. From there Ben then spent time at the remote Crinan Hotel in the West Highlands of Scotland where the supplier relationship was paramount and the only way to work was to be completely in tune with the seasons.

Returning to London, Ben joined the Salt Yard group, which focused on the cuisines of Spain and Italy, serving tapas-style dishes with a modern spin. As Chef Director he went onto open several award-winning restaurants with the group.

In 2018 Ben joined the Stafford London as their Culinary Director, overseeing the food at its Game Bird restaurant, the famous American Bar and its other outlets. 2019 will see Ben open a stand-alone restaurant with the Stafford focusing on Ben's love of southern Mediterranean and Moorish cooking.

This is Ben's third cookbook, having previously written *Salt Yard Food and Wine* (2012) and *Grill, Smoke, BBQ* (2016). He regularly appears on TV including shows such as *Saturday Kitchen*, *Masterchef* and *Sunday Brunch*.

Ben lives in East London with his wife Nykeeta and his French bulldog Piglet.

Acknowledgements

My brilliant and enthusiastic team at Absolute for not only believing in the project but understanding and getting behind it completely. Jon, Meg, Emily and Marie.

Kris Kirkham – my mate and the best food photographer I know. This is the second book I've worked with him on, alongside many other projects, and it's always so much fun, with always the best results.

My mates and fellow chefs, Roland Hector and Gianni Vatteroni, who gave their valuable time to help me with the photoshoot. It would not have been the result it is without you both.

Yvonne Poon, who gave her time for work experience and got us all in line on shoot days. She also made the best staff lunches!

Jason Atherton – chef and friend who has had a hand in much of my career and has been a constant supportive mentor.

Thanks to my friend and mentor David Ross, who I've had the pleasure of knowing for a relatively short while but a recent holiday with him to southern Italy has helped inspire this book. I hope to cook many dishes for him from within these pages.

My lovely wife, Nykeeta, and chief taster, Piglet the Frenchie, who have patience and enthusiasm in equal measures. I love you dearly.

My Dad, who unknowingly inspired me to be a chef with our left-field Friday steak nights 30 years ago; there was much flambéing involved and plenty of laughs!

Stuart Proctor, the inspirational GM at the Stafford Hotel, for reenergizing my love of the hospitality industry and his hilarious directness.

Jozef Rogulski, Jamie Thickett, Lidia Morales, Laszlo Nagy and Magda Kubanska – my very talented, hard-working senior chef team.

Jo Barnes and Martine Carter at Sauce Communications and Sauce Management respectively – there's not a better PR team.

My brilliant suppliers Wellocks, Walter Rose, Ginger Pig and Murray's Fresh Fish, whose fantastic produce you see on these pages.

Publisher
Jon Croft

Commissioning Editor
Meg Boas

Senior Editor
Emily North

Art Director & Designer
Marie O'Shepherd

Junior Designer
Anika Schulze

Production Controller
Marina Asenjo

Food Stylists
Ben Tish
Roland Hector
Yvonne Poon
Giancarlo Vatteroni

Photographer
Kris Kirkham
kriskirkhamphoto.com

Photographer's Assistant
Eyder Rosso Goncalves

Cartography
Emily Faccini

Copyeditor
Norma MacMillan

Home Economy
Adam O'Shepherd

Proofreader
Kate Moore

Indexer
Zoe Ross

BLOOMSBURY ABSOLUTE
Bloomsbury Publishing Plc
50 Bedford Square, London, WC1B 3DP, UK
29 Earlsfort Terrace, Dublin 2, Ireland

BLOOMSBURY, BLOOMSBURY ABSOLUTE, the Diana logo and the
Absolute Press logo are trademarks of Bloomsbury Publishing Plc

First published in Great Britain 2019

Bloomsbury Publishing Plc does not have any control over, or
responsibility for, any third-party websites referred to or in this book. All
internet addresses given in this book were correct at the time of going
to press. The author and publisher regret any inconvenience caused if
addresses have changed or sites have ceased to exist, but can accept no
responsibility for any such changes.

A catalogue record for this book is available from the British Library.
Library of Congress Cataloguing-in-Publication data has been applied for.

HB: 9781472958075
ePub: 9781472958068
ePDF: 9781472958082

4 6 8 10 9 7 5 3

Printed and bound in China by C&C Offset Printing Co., Ltd.

Bloomsbury Publishing Plc makes every effort to ensure that the papers
used in the manufacture of our books are natural, recyclable products
made from wood grown in well-managed forests. Our manufacturing
processes conform to the environmental regulations of the country
of origin.

To find out more about our authors and books visit www.bloomsbury.com
and sign up for our newsletters.